BOILER SUITS,
BOFORS AND BULLE

Edited by Jenny Edgar, Literature Development Officer, Derbyshire County Council, with Kath Housley, Doris Flint, Kath Boxall and Edna Tomlinson.

First Published 1999 by
Derbyshire County Council
Libraries and Heritage Department.
County Hall,
Matlock,
Derbyshire DE4 3AG

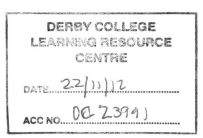

ISBN 0 903463 57 1
© 1999 Photographs by Nigel Tissington
© 1999 Photographs Robert Opie on pages 16, 20, 21, 24, 41, 44, 45, 48, 85, 89, 96, 109, 116, 117, 128
© 1999 Front Cover Design, Layout and Print by Dick Richardson, Country Books.

Title page:
Enjoying the E.N.S.A. Concert at Collaro Ltd. 16th June 1944.

'Boiler Suits, Bofors and Bullets' has been published with financial assistance from Derbyshire County Council, Libraries and Heritage Department, East Midlands Arts, and Amber Valley Borough Council.

In 1939 a firm manufacturing munitions in Peckham, South London was bombed out of their factory for the second time. In an attempt to avoid German bombers they moved to Vic Hallam's factory at Langley Mill. The firm was called Collaro and its arrival in the quiet village had an immense impact on the lives of local people, not only from Langley Mill but also surrounding towns and villages.

Young women who worked in lingerie and lace factories found themselves in a massive factory producing bullets and machine pieces. Low wages were replaced by the chance to earn good money, more than their fathers and brothers earned down the pit.

But who would work the lace machines and the seamers now that the young women had gone to work with the Londoners who'd come up with Collaro's? How would boyfriends and husbands react to their girlfriends and wives not only earning a living but a very good one? When the war was over and peace was declared would they all settle back to the old life? Soldiers had spent years away from their families and girls and boys had courted not in the local cinema but through letters that were defaced with the censor's pen.

At the end of the war Collaro's returned to London, Vic Hallam once again took over his factory and life returned to something approaching normal. Nothing was ever written down about the men and women, the workers, who were the driving force of the Collaro factory.

Nearly sixty years after Collaro's opened in Langley Mill a gift of a photograph album was made to Heanor Library. It's owner, Mr. Christopher, a manager at Collaro's, had recently died and his daughter felt the history within the album might be of interest to local people. One of those people, Elaine Glenwright, Deputy District Librarian, had a particular interest. Her mother had been one of the young women who'd put on the boiler suit, tucked her hair into a turban and worked on the machinery making ammunition. Elaine suggested the experiences of those workers should be recorded and from this grew the Collaro Project.

From October 1st. 1998 a group of ex-Collaro employees met at Heanor Library to talk or write of their experiences. Those teenagers are now in their seventies and for many it was the first time they had met since they all went their separate ways at the end of the war.

The Library has been as far removed as could be imagined from the 'Silence Please' notices that were in evidence when these people used the library in their young days. It has been alive with memories, clear and detailed, that have flooded back as they've talked together.

This book is a compilation of those memories and every person who attended the meetings is represented here.

Jenny Edgar
Literature Development Officer.
Derbyshire County Council.

6 · CONTRIBUTORS

Married names are in brackets.

Kath Ainsworth	(Adcock)
Kath Eley	(Boxall)
Vera	(Brewster)
Betty Sumner	(Cook)
Joan Brown	(Cuttell)
Ivy Carmen	(Cross)
Enid Briggs	(Dunnett)
May	(Elwell)
Betty Brown	(England)
Doris Brewin	(Flint)
Betty	(Hartle)
Annie Morse	(Henshaw)
Vera	(Hutchinson)
Kath Gilbert	(Housley)
Len Kirby	
Alice Parkin	(Kirkman)
Madge Hill	(McIver)
Clara	(Middleton)
M. Neale	
Jack Otterwell	
Olive	(Otterwell)
Joyce Berrisford	(Owen)
Hilda	(Parker)
Joyce	(Parr)
Frances	(Palmer)
Gladys Swindell	(Radford)
Brenda Hallows	(Robinson)
Lois Palmer	(Shaw)
Edna	(Tomlinson)
Phyllis Unwin	(Watson)
Jessie Watson	(Purdy)
W. Woolley	

The group were saddened by the deaths of Annie Morse (nee Henshaw), Betty Hartle and Vera Brewster. They had been enthusiastic and involved members of the group and our thanks go to their widowers, Mr. Henshaw and Mr. Hartle and the family of Vera Brewster for allowing us to include Annie, Betty and Vera's memories.

The Collaro Group would like to thank the following people:
Jeanne Dall, Fay Jones and Sue Needham, librarians at Heanor Library, and Derek Fox for their interest and good humour when collecting memories; Eve Fox and other library staff for making the group so welcome; East Midlands Arts, Derbyshire County Council and Amber Valley Borough Council who have helped the project in many ways, including providing the financial support necessary to publish the book; special thanks to Jaci Brumwell, Deputy Director of Libraries and Heritage, Derbyshire County Council, Sue Stewart, Literature Officer, East Midlands Arts and Vicki Campbell, Arts Officer with Amber Valley Borough Council for their continued interest and support.

1: *September Song*

Kurt Weill

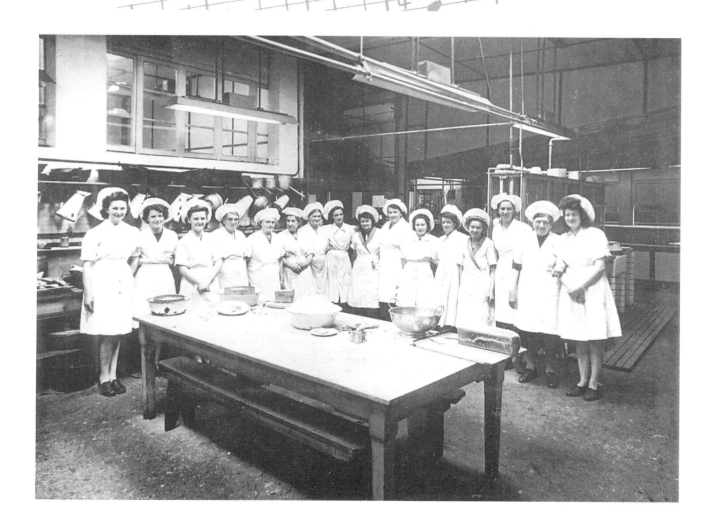

Langley Mill lies in a valley between Eastwood and Heanor bounded by the River Erewash and the Old Canal. Years ago the River Erewash flowed under the main road and at this point was not much more than a briskly running stream. Come a period of heavy rain or snow it very quickly changed character and flooding was commonplace on Cromford Road and into the low-lying fields adjoining the route of the canal. The water also came further up into the village as far as the bridges carrying the main railway lines.

There was a whirlpool too. Poorly fenced, it was an ever-present danger. In later years it was filled and piped away but not before it had claimed the lives of many children. The water-wheel which powered Smith's Flour Mill on Cromford Road was out of bounds too.

In the thirties and forties the area was a mix of the rural and industrial. Coal mining was the main source of work along with farming, engineering, rolling stock production, a pottery and a hosiery factory owned by Aristoc, Ltd. It flourished but the down-side was the amount of debris that was the result of such activities. The mines had wastes of stone, slate and coal dust that was deposited onto ever-growing 'pit hills', continually combusting and reeking of sulphuric smoke. The steam powered railways, both Northern and Midland lines, linked up to branch lines to the pits with sidings to the heavy industrial engineering works and foundries.

We had coal fires at home and the resultant smoke gathered in the valley, hemmed in by the high ground on all sides and formed a fog that wasn't helped by smoke from the factories.

In this mixture of country and town we walked the fields and breathed in smoky air, played by the river and watched the miners, caked in coal dust, walk home from the pits.

The tram to Heanor Market on Friday night, just Mum and me; to the Meadow Dairy for butter patted to shape with sunny meadows and cows plump and horned. Woolworth's was a magic kingdom and the promise of a jigsaw puzzle for good behaviour kept me in order. At the back of the market was a shop that sold cow-heels, tripe and cooked pigs feet. Nearby was a fresh fish shop with a gleaming marble sloped slab where ice and parsley

The Collaro Ltd. kitchen and canteen staff 1944-45.

kept the goods damp. It was always quite possible that the brown paper bags would disintegrate and you'd be left with just the string handles!

We had a single storey cinema called the Picture House. The best and most expensive seats were three steps up. At Christmas the management gave every child an apple and an orange. A piano was played for sorrow or anger, real 'mood music'. Programmes changed twice weekly and cost sixpence a seat and a free ticket to the Saturday matinee for children.

With the coming of the talkies we had a new cinema called 'The Ritz'. This was really 'something' with carpeted floors and a proper balcony. I have vivid memories of seeing 'Uncle Tom's Cabin' when Little Ella crossed the breaking ice with a baby clutched in her arms. I trod every dangerous step with her whilst sobbing my socks off!

I went to school at the top of the street. The school's still going, but as a school for infants not Sedgwick Street Girls' School as it was then. High windows, dark green and brown paint with a little bit of cream stuck up at the top. Painted brick walls and a coal fire in each class. They were quite big classrooms so you can imagine we were always warm on one side if we were lucky enough to sit near the fire. Not only the building was Victorian. We were all terrified of the teachers. I don't think anybody dare say 'boo' to a goose.

" I often used to walk to meet Dad from Shipley Pit. I loved his dirty face and hands. Mum would have the tin bath in front of the fire full of hot water from the coal boiler. "

Home was the centre of everything and we spent a lot of time with our families. Not many mothers worked outside the home, they'd got enough to do bringing us up, so they were always there. And we had our jobs to do too because housework and cooking were hard work. No hot water, a boiler for washing clothes and heavy flat irons that had to be heated up on the range.

Mother always had the kettle on. Always. You never had to wait for it to boil. Everyone had ranges with a coal fire in the middle and an oven to one

side. Most Saturday nights Mum would put leg-meat in a large brown stew pot in the coal oven and leave it to stew all night. I loved the smell! We had it for Sunday morning breakfast. We used to think there were stars on the top. A dish each with a thick slice of dry bread — delicious.

Mum was very good at making a little go a long way and she would mix our best butter with margarine, which was blocked, hard margarine, then with some hot milk till it was nice and creamy.

She used to buy large marrowbones from the butcher, boil them, let them cool and skim the fat off. It made lovely pastry.

We always had home made bread and cakes. Dad was the one who made the bread. But it was a real treat if we had a cream cake. On a Saturday morning Spendlove's cake shop would sell their broken cream cakes cheap, but you had to be early in a morning and queue for a bag of half a dozen. Broken or not they were lovely.

" The farmer at the top of Monument Hill kept a pig and my Mum bought half of it and we used to fetch the meat when we wanted it. It was a luxury. "

There wasn't time to be bored as it was a case of helping out with housework when your day's work was done. There'd be cleaning to do and there was always ironing to be finished with the flat irons. I've spent many an evening waiting for them to heat up. I didn't think anything of it because by the time I was twenty my Mum had two more children and it was a case of there being even more work to do.

I loved clothes. Not that I had many. Or needed them, come to that. We worked long hours and didn't have the time to go out much. What we did have we looked after. It was a case of having to. And we always kept one lot of clothes for Sundays.

My sister and I were always proud of our 'Sunday Best Dresses'. We were only allowed to wear them on 'High Days and Holidays' and for Chapel. Woe betide us if we got them dirty or torn so as soon as we were back home

Joan and Betty Brown.

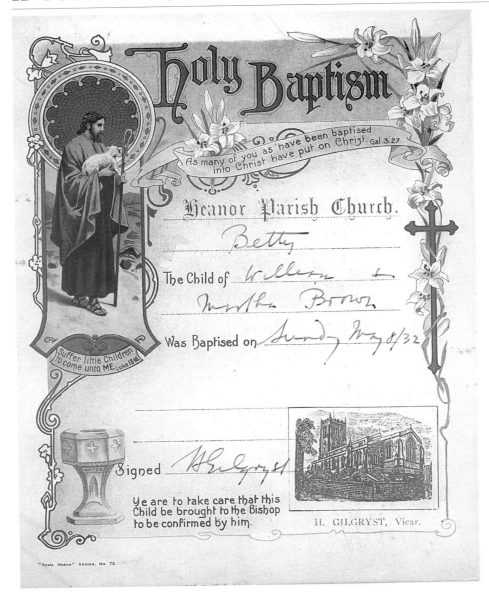

Betty Brown's baptismal certificate.

we had to change into old clothes before we went out to play. I suppose they were extra-special because a lot of our clothes were hand-me-downs.

Up to leaving school all girls had to wear a Liberty Bodice, socks and knickers, usually navy, that were changed every other day. When cami-knickers came into fashion I couldn't wait to wear a pair. They seemed so sexy. Then I worried in case the buttons popped off between my legs. It would have made it feel a bit draughty.

When we started work Mum let us go into vests and more 'feminine' underwear with suspender belts to hold up our stockings. That's if you were lucky enough to be able to buy a pair. The girls used to go crazy for a pair of stockings.

Our skirts were worn just below the knee with short-sleeved blouses and jumpers. Cardigans that buttoned up to the neck were all the rage and I've even worn them back-to-front just for a change. Once my sister and I wore pyjama tops to a skirt just because they were pretty.

Whenever our family needed shoes repairing my Dad used to mend them on a shoe hob he kept on a bench in the shed. Teenagers wouldn't go out dancing or on a date with flat shoes on and out would come your stiletto-heeled shoes. I for one wouldn't wear anything but a high heel for a date. In fact I had a craze on shoes and would buy a pair whenever I could afford them. It was one of my weaknesses.

If it was a wet or windy day we wore scarves on our heads to protect our hair. Chiffon ones were my favourite.

The men used to wear stiff, starched collars with long points. My mother used to wash about thirty a week. Then they'd fasten them with collar studs onto Granddad shirts and ties were a must. Most men wore suits or flannels and sports coats, usually 'Made to Measure' from 'Burton's Tailoring'. Only people with plenty of cash to spare went to the more expensive tailor's shops.

Flared trousers were the favourite with buttoned fly-fronts. No zips then. And they were held up with braces. A long raincoat and a Trilby or a flat cap were what the best dressed young men used to wear. There were no short socks then, they were all knee length and held up with suspenders.

Most houses only had one coal fire to heat the whole house so warmth was a must. I think I knitted every male in our family a Fair Isle waistcoat.

Money was tight and at fourteen we left school to earn our livings. Our money mattered. We 'tipped-up' every pay-day and were given back some pocket money to last us the week. The rest went into the housekeeping.

" I worked at Hampshire's, the pharmaceutical factory at Riddings, who made face creams, powder, rouge and the 'Snowfire' tablet which was a good remedy for chapped hands and feet, and still is today. "

Before the outbreak of war I was working at Aristoc making pure silk stockings. No nylons then. After a while I went on to a linking machine that joined the seams of the heels and toes of the stockings together ready for the seamers. I loved the work and because I lived just across the road I had no buses to catch. I was very handy when any orders came in for export. The Boss over me, a Mr. Barnsdall, would send for me to help out whether it was holiday time or not, but I willingly obliged as it was extra money. It was very welcome. I was the oldest of three children and times were very hard.

I worked from a quarter-past-seven in the morning to a quarter-past-five at night and Saturday mornings for nine shillings and nine-pence.

Everyone knew the war was going to happen and people were sent to different factories to work on war goods. I was sent to Ericson's at Beeston where tele-communications were being made for the Forces. I had to leave home at six o'clock to catch the six-fifteen train. We never knew when we'd be shunted into a siding to allow Government Transport and Troop movements.

Aristoc stopped making stockings and went into Barrage balloon work so back I went to be nearer home. The 'Floor Gangs' we were called. All the work was done on our hands and knees, scrubbing the silver off the fabric so that stabilizers could be stuck on. We wore bib-and-brace overalls and knee-pads. We had to use glue that was foul-smelling and clung to us as if it was another skin.

We all got on very well. I knew a lot of the girls because I was at school with them and it was a time of great companionship. We were a hardworking lot

of girls. It was great. My pocket money was one and sixpence a week and we made sure we had threepence in case there was a collection for anybody getting married and threepence for Church collection. Afterwards when we earned more and our pocket money was increased we were able to save a little and buy clothes. More often than not I gave my mother a helping hand with money as it was always a case of being short by about Thursday. They were very happy days and there was a wonderful spirit.

We needed that spirit to see us through the next six years. Even though we knew the war was not just a likelihood but almost definitely going to happen it was difficult to believe that our lives would change so dramatically. We used to laugh with Robb Wilton, a famous radio comedian, who based his humour on the phrase 'The day war broke out...' little knowing how devastating the next few years would be.

That Sunday morning, September 3rd. 1939, was bright, warm and sunny. We hurried to finish the Sunday lunch chores so that we could listen to Mr. Chamberlain's broadcast as a family. For my Mother and Father it was a shattering blow. Their memories of 1914 –18 were still vivid and dreadful, and my newly married sister and her husband, my brother and I were stunned and disbelieving. To make matters worse within the hour the air-raid sirens wailed over us and I for one wondered if we were going to be bombed and homeless, if not killed by the end of the day.

What should we do? Get under the table? Go down the pantry steps? Draw the curtains to stop flying glass? Before we had any answers the 'All Clear' sounded. Just testing after all.

We were all a bit scared. After all we weren't that old. Just bits of kids really. We used to spread rugs and coats on the cellar steps so that we'd got somewhere to sit when the sirens went. Sometimes we were absolutely petrified but other times it was just boring. I've spent hours waiting for the 'All Clear'.

And the gas masks. They were horrible things, the rubber used to stick to your face. The smaller children liked them though. They realised that if you took a deep breath and then blew out hard you could make a rude noise with the rubber vibrating against your skin. We had to carry them everywhere in a little square box. And babies had a sort of carrying-box gas mask. They were completely encased in this shell. We never had to use them but we had plenty of practises.

From then on our lives changed. Blackout curtains were compulsory, rationing was introduced and we all knew when the sweet allocation had arrived. A large queue formed and coupons from ration books were handed in. What a treat!

" I used to travel on a train with only the split lamps for lighting. They were almost one candle power. "

There was a programme on the radio called 'Radio Allotment' and a 'Dig for Victory' campaign. Households dug up their lawns and set potatoes and other vegetables and a quarter-of-a-million allotments were developed from parks and gardens. They provided ten percent of our food during the war. Not much food was shipped to England. My Dad kept half a dozen hens at the top of our garden. This helped out a lot but there were six in our family so we didn't all get an egg each. No one ever complained. After all we were lucky compared with The Forces.

Although food was rationed and scarce we never went hungry. Most homes had to use dried egg powder and dried milk because there was never enough fresh eggs and milk to go around. It was very, very plain. No luxuries. If you'd got a mother who was very organised and could make a meal out of nothing you were all right. We had the usual things. Usual for then. Tins of spam and corned beef hash, that sort of thing. But we managed. Whenever we could we'd contribute food at the Town Hall or other centres to be packed up in food parcels for the Forces.

" When my Mum had the bacon ration she used to wrap a slice of bacon and an egg or sausage and put my name on it. The canteen staff would cook it and it would be ready for break time. It was delicious. "

Times were grim but they were nothing in comparison to what the boys in the forces were facing. We stayed at home and waited and that was bad enough but they had to leave everything behind and go and fight.

My brother went into the Army. He was only eighteen and he'd never been beyond Derby. Six weeks training, that's all he had, then he went off to India. It was a terrible shock because he'd never been anywhere, done anything. Anybody from away was a foreigner. It was quite an adventure to go to Nottingham or Sheffield.

One night in 1940 I had made arrangements to meet my husband on Derby bus station. He was stationed at Allestree Hall for a month or two. I arranged to go straight from work and we thought we'd go for a meal. It would be about six o'clock when I got there. I waited for an hour but my husband never turned up. It turned out he had to go on smoke screens and there was no way he could have let me know. In the meantime there was a soldier standing a little way away from me. As I waited for each bus to come in, so did he. Eventually he came up to me and said 'It looks as if the both of us have been let down.' We spoke for a few minutes and I said I was famished. I told him I had come straight from work to meet my husband and that we were going to go for some chips. He said 'Well — why not come and do the same with me.' I did and caught the eight-thirty bus back from Derby, the last one. We exchanged names and addresses and wrote to one another for a couple of years. I suppose he eventually went abroad. Anyway I told my husband all about it. He wasn't very pleased at first but eventually the letters stopped. I never knew what happened to him.

My husband and a friend had their embarkation leave and then were on their way. Shortly afterwards I had a letter from this friend's wife telling me where my husband and hers were going to. They had made a pact that he would mention a certain thing and after that the first letter of each sentence would spell out the name of the ship and where it was off to. It turned out it was the Britannia and was on its way to India. He eventually went to Northern India and Burma. Unfortunately my friend's husband never came

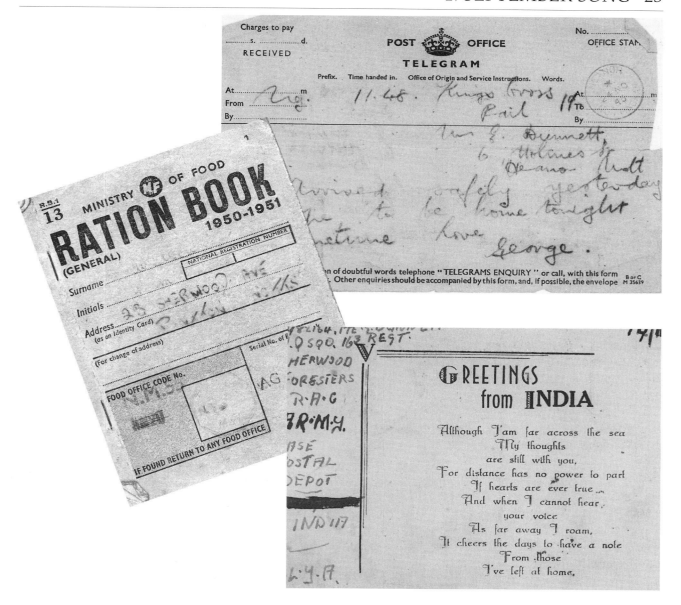

back. I was lucky, my husband did come back but was never as well as he'd been before he went.

The war had really begun and our lives were going to be changed for ever. Two hundred miles away in Peckham, South London, the Collaro factory had been bombed for the second time. Before the war they'd manufactured gramophone turn-tables but they turned to making ammunition. Vic Hallam, our local timber merchant, had to leave his factory so that Collaro could set up in Langley Mill. We'd never even heard of 'Collaro' never mind thought about working for them. We didn't know it but we were going to work very hard in terrible conditions and earn money that our fathers could only dream of. And we'd cement friendships that would last us a lifetime.

2: *I'll Never Be The Same*

By Frank Signorelli & Matt Malneck.

The marriage of a manufacturer of gramophone turn-tables and the local timber merchant seemed a most unlikely way to spawn a highly organised munitions factory. But it did. They brought experienced workers with them who taught us the work, lived with our families, became part of Langley Mill. Some never did go home to London.

We were bombed during the early days of the Blitz. It was made worse because the railway line to the South Coast ran behind the factory and they were aiming for both targets. The government decided to evacuate us and found a new factory that had just been built by Vic Hallam at Langley Mill. We wondered if it was in a different country!

Anyway my Dad and myself came up to Nottingham on two weekends to find somewhere for the family to live. We found a house on Nottingham Road — 'Hill Top' — it had been a private school at one time.

All the machines that were workable were brought up on lorries, put into their positions and set working as soon as possible. We couldn't afford to waste time.

We started to employ some of the local people, young lads, girls, married women. Those young lads were lucky they didn't get the reception I got on my first day. There I was, a lad of fourteen, being stripped naked by the female workers and greased and oiled from head to toe!

The local folk couldn't make up their minds about us. We were foreigners. It showed up when we got on the bus to go home; they shifted away from us because we smelt of oil.

" It came as a bit of a shock when the firm came from London. I suppose it brought the war a bit nearer to us. "

Most of the work force, of course, were London people and had horrifying tales to tell of being bombed out. I think they thought we were very lucky not knowing any of that. Mind you the Londoners couldn't tell what we were saying and vice versa. The London twang grated and the swearing seemed unending. To be fair I don't think I felt sorry for their situation for a long time, not until news came through of the bombing. They lost parents, homes and friends who'd stayed down there. Then I saw their grief.

My mother took one of the workmen from London as a lodger. That meant my nine-year old brother had to give up his room and sleep in with my parents. I remember Mr. Palmer very well. He was middle-aged and very quiet. His wife and children had been evacuated to Wales and during one school holiday my mother invited them to stay because she felt sorry that they were parted. It was chaos. Everyone had to be shuffled round and my parents slept downstairs.

It was a difficult time for everyone. We didn't have much choice about what we did. It was either The Forces or Collaro's and my parents didn't want me to go away so Collaro's it was.

" Our boss was so annoyed with us for leaving. My friend was one of his favourites, you see. We gave our notice in on the Friday morning and by the afternoon he'd given us two weeks wages and told us we could leave there and then. "

I can't explain the feeling of leaving a job I really enjoyed and going to a place that was alien to me. At the first it was really traumatic. The man on the gates gave me such a look. Funnily enough, after a while, we all got to like him. I think he was sorry for girls having to do war work but that first morning he scared me silly.

I was terrified by the sight and noise of those enormous machines, never dreaming I was eventually going to have to work one. So many different things to cope with. We had clocking in cards, something I'd never had to use at the hosiery factory and if you were one minute late it cost you fifteen minutes wages. We were issued with a Khaki boiler suit and a cap. That took some getting used to but they were the very things to wear for the work we were going to be doing. Each week we'd go along to the canteen and swop our dirty boiler suit for a clean one. Just once a week. And they were dirty.

In those days if you were told to do something you did it without question. The foreman on the inspection benches, a tall, thin man with black hair and eyes to match, put the fear of God into me! If he stood behind me I daren't move or speak. One of the most frightening parts of the job, apart from working a big machine, was the fact that men were telling me what to do. I'd not been used to it. The fitters patrolled up and down, keeping an eye, making sure the machines were in full working order. The fact was it was work that had to be done and we got on with it. The bosses used to do their rounds, coming and inspecting the work we turned out and, on the whole, as long as you didn't waste time, they were pretty fair.

Anyone walking into the factory just saw rows of benches where they made gramophone pick-ups so no-one would know what the real business was. When you got further in it was ammunitions. It was a long factory with wide double benches with girls packed either side in a continuous assembly line; testing, checking with gauges, painting lids with red oxide and using hand presses to seal them into a tiny screw-sided nut. It was never fully explained to us exactly what we were making and I never saw a fully assembled war-head of the shell case.

The work was for the C.I.A, the Chief Inspector of Armaments, and our boss, Mr. Christopher from London, was a real gentleman. We nicknamed the C.I.A 'Churchill's Idle Army'!!!

❝ There wasn't much about the interview except standing in the office and looking out over the factory floor with my knees knocking. That I remember. ❞

On the very first day Mabel, the overlooker, came around saying 'It's overtime tonight till 8pm.' It nearly killed us. We used to be in such a hurry to get home at night. To save time Mabel used to stand working the clocking-out machine. The buses were so full in those days. If they got a chance they would hurry past Collaro's so they wouldn't have to pick us up. We'd race up to the next stop nearer Eastwood and we'd just catch the bus by the skin of our teeth, sometimes just hanging on, and the driver would speed up on purpose.

Word got around that it was more money if you worked nights so we

*Collaro Ltd. Inspection benches
+ "60" New Britains.*

volunteered. We were only sixteen years old and you had to be eighteen really. Gosh, we only managed one week then we went back on long days. We'd had enough of that.

We'd started on a Sunday night shift and I thought it was absolutely awful having to work on a Sunday. This was the night we used to walk on the town to meet the boys, have a chat and then they'd walk us home. I thought it was the end of my life!! For me the daytime was still for doing things just as I had before. I thought I could manage with little sleep. So I met friends in the morning, went for a walk, then went to bed to try and sleep. Yes, it did come, sleep, but it was soon time to catch the 7 o'clock bus and start all over again.

I didn't know I was on a bonus so when I got my first wage I went to the wages office and told them I had been paid too much. I was told never to discuss my wages with anyone as we were all paid differently depending on what job we were doing.

The machines were very complicated to begin with but with time we got into the rhythm of working them and became very competent. There were about six different operations to do consisting of drilling, facing and tapping. It was a very tiring job but we had to do it for twelve hours at a time. There were two of us to a machine and we used to take it in turns to operate and inspect the work.

> **" The contrast between working environments was a real shock. From a warm, dry atmosphere we were working on rough pebbled floors of concrete. "**

For some of us working at Collaro's was a way of showing people what we could do. In those days girls weren't expected to have a career. They took a job, any job, until they married and had babies. That was what was expected of them.

I was a rebel. That's why I ended up at Collaro's. Most of my friends had gone to work at 'Aristoc' making stockings but I didn't want to be like everyone else.

I think it was all tied up with not going to Grammar School. I wasn't one of the brightest ones at school but when we were in the last year a certain few of us were in the top ten which meant you were more or less expected to go to Grammar School. My maths weren't brilliant but I was good at English, History, things like that. When the time came they used to give you forms to take home for your parents to sign where they'd agree to you taking the test. There was no point. It just wasn't on the cards, that's all. They just couldn't afford it. There was uniform to buy, all the books and equipment and my father was working in the pit on low wages. My mother was never well enough to go out to work, never very strong, so it just wasn't going to happen. I don't think it crossed my mind that I could go. I was a bit disappointed but a lot of my personal friends didn't go either so it didn't upset me too much at the time. It was later on, in my teens, when I realised that I should have gone. Just before I left school I had an idea I'd like to go to business college. One of my cousins had gone to do a secretarial course, shorthand and typing, that sort of thing. She started to teach me shorthand and I got interested in it and said I'd like to go. I couldn't because we'd have had to pay.

As my brother got older he was allowed to do all the things I hadn't. But he didn't go to Grammar School because he wasn't bright enough. That was just the thing, you see. He'd never had the chance, there was no question of him going, but if he had been bright enough he'd have been allowed to. Things were better then, it was after the war and we were much better off. That sort of thing did rankle.

I never talked to my Mum and Dad about it, never blamed them. I didn't think it was their fault, or anything like that.

In those days it wasn't considered important to educate a girl. We'd get married, have babies and that was that.

When I was eleven it was the early thirties and the pits weren't working. It was a real slump, really bad. My dad used to get up at half-past four and walk to Loscoe pit. That was about three or four miles to get to the face they were working on. They'd get right down there and then be told they weren't working it that day so they'd turn around and come all the way back. I began to cotton on to what my mother was listening for. You could hear all the miners with their pit boots on, like an army on the march, coming back from across the fields and the main road, and before nine o'clock when I had to go to school my Dad was back home. No money, nothing for all that. It used to go on for weeks at a time, just a day or half a day. So what chance was there of me going to Grammar School?

What I really wanted was to work in an office. To start with I went into the factory, everybody did, making those little — what do you call them — ferrules? Yes, that's it. But my older sister was working in the offices and when a vacancy came up in the wages department she put me up for it. I stayed there until they closed.

It wasn't long before Vic Hallam's factory wasn't big enough to hold us all and with so many workers on night and day shifts we badly needed a canteen. There was an old pub in the factory grounds, the New Inn, and that was kitted out as our works canteen. We thought we'd been busy before but things speeded up even more.

❝ My grandma was in the canteen, my Dad was one of the storekeepers and I had three cousins who worked there. ❞

We'd started to get new machines from America and Canada that came in big wooden crates. Everyone wanted a crate. They made great garden sheds! At the same time we were getting steel and aluminium from America to produce the armour piercing shell and nose fuse for the Bofor anti-aircraft shells. They had thirty-seven parts in them and we made nearly all of them. The smallest part was called a needle. It was too small to check properly and had to be magnified one hundred times on what was called a shadow-graph. And we made a tracer body and land mine striker pin.

Eventually production had risen so much that the factory was too small so it was extended to over double its original size. They built air raid shelters

too and we had the odd occasion to use these, especially when the bus garage on Mansfield Road was hit.

'Music While You Work' was piped throughout the factory and did it boost our morale! We'd got a lot of good singers amongst us and we'd hear them effortlessly hitting the high notes over and above the incessant noise of the machinery. It was wonderful. Certain songs were allocated to certain warblers and a count was made of the number of times they were played in a week. We organized our own 'Top of the Pops' and joined in.

We had lovely concerts, 'Workers' Playtime' with the professionals and we used to put them on ourselves on Friday nights. There were lovely turns. The man who was in charge came round asking 'What can you do?' My friend who was on the machine with me said 'She's in the choir, she can sing.' So I sang a duet with another girl of 'I'll See You Again'. And there was a father and daughter that worked in the plating shop who sang beautifully. Songs of the day, wartime songs. And there was a man that played the mouth organ. There were little prizes for whoever was the best.

Once a month we had a dance. That was marvellous, trying to dance on the canteen floor. That was great. I really enjoyed it.

We'd put a dustbin lid in the middle of the floor and throw money in. That went for comforts for The Forces.

In some ways Collaro's was a little world on its own. But home life still went on, we went dancing, courted, got on with living.

I met my husband because I couldn't afford to turn up for my other date! I was going up to Leabrooks to go dancing with this lad but when the night came I hadn't got enough money to go out. No-one would lend me any but I though 'Well — I'm not stopping in'.

One of the girls at work had made a date with a lad called Ron and I turned up to see him instead! That was it, that was the one I married.

We had to go to Chapel on a Sunday, three times a day. I finished up being a Sunday School teacher because it was the only way you could get out on a

Early One Morning

Early one morning, just as the sun was rising,
I heard a maid sing in the valley below:
'Oh, don't deceive me; oh, never leave me!
How could you use a poor maiden so?'

'Oh, gay is the garland, and fresh are the roses,
I've cull'd from the garden to bind on thy brow'.
'Oh, don't deceive me; oh, never leave me!
How could you use a poor maiden so?'

Remember the vows that you made to your Mary,
Remember the bow'r where you vow'd to be true.
'Oh, don't deceive me; oh, never leave me!
How could you use a poor maiden so?'

Thus sang the poor maiden, her sorrows bewailing,
Thus sang the maid in the valley below:
'Oh, don't deceive me; oh, never leave me!
How could you use a poor maiden so?'

Sunday. Straight after chapel we'd take a quick whip round the corner and there they were! On the Monkey Run. The boys would walk one way round the square, the girls the other. Funnily enough you always seemed to find a blonde and a brunette in pairs in those days. If you didn't go on the monkey run you didn't live.

> **" I've spent hours on Heanor Rec chatting up the boys. "**

After the twelve hour shifts we would sleep for four hours then get changed and go roller-skating at Nottingham, to the cinema at Ripley or dancing at The Palais. It was lovely to change out of boiler suits into a normal dress but clothes were hard to come by. Everything was on coupons. It was handy being able to make your own clothes. I was a sewing-machinist before working at Collaro's so I made myself one or two dresses. Mind you, my Dad thought it was wrong for me to go dancing after working twelve-hour shifts but I got my energy somehow and it made life more interesting. Things were so dark and drab during the blackouts. There was not much to laugh about in those days. You had to have some fun somehow.

Just one fly in the ointment was having to come home in the blackout. All the train windows were blacked and the stations were in darkness, so I had to count the stops between Chesterfield and Langley Mill so as not to miss my station. I was scared stiff of going by because the next stop was in the middle of nowhere!

Our spare time wasn't just to enjoy ourselves. The war effort meant everyone had to do their bit.

Where once there'd been green lawns were rows of potatoes. Anyone with a garden grew their own fruit and vegetables to eke out the rations of meat and cheese. Parks and gardens lost their iron rails and fences; the metal was needed to be melted down along with piles of old saucepans that people donated.

In big cities and towns barrage balloons were erected to deter enemy

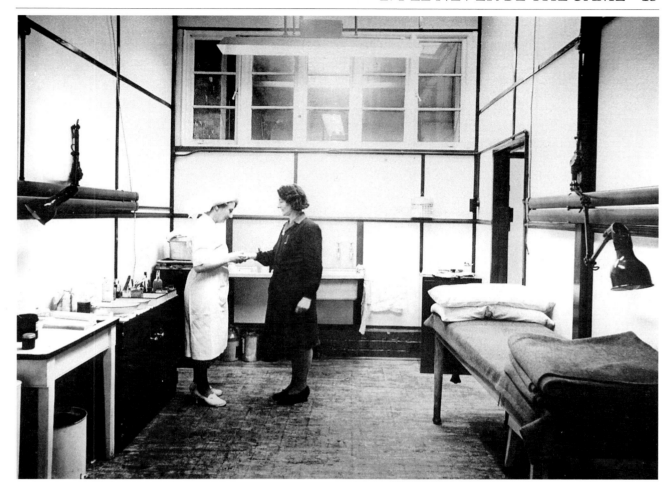

The surgery, Collaro Ltd.
1944-45.

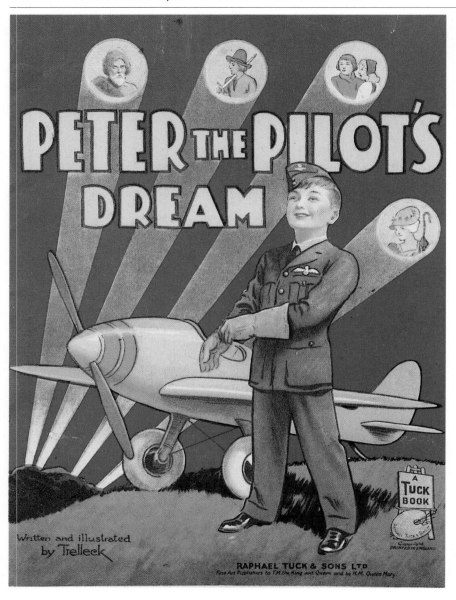

aircraft. From Heanor you could clearly see the search lights over Derby during a raid. We would listen to the drone of aircraft waiting for Dad to say 'It's okay. It's one of ours.'

> **" The London workforce didn't mix very well with us. They thought we were all thick and talked funny. "**

As we got to know the London girls better and realised how lonely and homesick they were we began to invite them home for a meal. Of course we all had a lot in common with sweethearts and husbands away in The Forces. That made a difference.

Even though we were severely rationed my Mother, God bless her, always baked bread and pies and cakes, despite having to use the dreaded dried egg. One of my uncles had a piggery in production for the government and was allowed to rear several pigs for his family. We used to benefit from his generosity. A ham hung in the pantry from a huge hook; slabs of home-cured bacon, mostly fat, and pork dripping by the basin-full always with gorgeous brown jelly at the bottom. Nectar! Delicious with home-made bread and salt.

> **" I lived the other side of Heanor so it was such a rush to get back up the hill, especially if we had broth for dinner. It didn't half make you sweat! "**

At times it seemed as if we could forget there was a war going on but there was another side to it with casualties both at home and abroad.

My friend Annie had a terrible time. She'd recently got married and not long after she had a telegram from the War Office. Her husband was stationed in Kent and his hut had been hit with a doodlebug. He suffered terrible injuries and died soon after she got down there.

Then she found she was pregnant and the baby was born fit and healthy but the heartbreak was too much for Annie. She died soon after.

We had a collection and everybody rallied round and gave as much as

they could. We bought the baby a lovely pram and accessories. I shall never forget how she put on a brave face in spite of suffering so much heartache.

" One day they came to tell us that from then on we had to give up our clothing coupons if we wanted a new overall. It nearly caused a riot as the coupons were so precious but I can't remember if anything came of it. "

I wore a scarf as a turban instead of my peaked cap. It looked more feminine. If we were working on the drills we certainly had to make sure all of our hair was covered. One night there was this awful scream. One of the girls working on the drills had left her hair free and it had got caught in the machine. It ripped it out. Right out.

Late 1940 was a time of great change and upheaval and a time of growing up very quickly. Up until that time the war was called 'The Phoney War'. But it changed. It wasn't phoney any more.

All around us boys and girls we'd grown up with were going into the Forces to reappear as Rear Gunners, Observers, Pilots, Air Gunners, Naval and Army Personnel, Nurses and Ambulance Drivers.

Refugees arrived from London and other cities which were bombed. It was heartbreaking to see very young children, complete with a box containing a gas mask, a small parcel and a label with their name and home address pinned on their clothes, being led in groups from the stations. So many were crying and looking totally bereft of hope.

The day my brother died I got home from work and I couldn't understand what was happening. My Mum was prostrate. I think the shock had been so great that Mum and Dad couldn't talk, they were just busy with each other. Mum was in a terrible state. My sister and my auntie were there and during the time from me coming home from work and asking if I could go out most of my mother's brothers and sisters turned up so there was a house full. I

TO:- Lpl. G. Dunnett 4388 64   521054
Spec Coy
13th Btn Sherwood Foresters
India Command

Write the message very plainly below this line.

Sender's Address: Mrs. G. Dunnett, 6 Holmes St Heanor, Notts

My Dear George,
I hope you like
this photograph of
Phil and myself
I think it's
marvelous of Phil
it shows what a
little man he gets
Its a pity I couldn't
send it the size
it is now instead
of it having to
be photographed
Well heres all
my love & Phels
hoping you
receive it safely

Your ever loving wife & son.

This space should not be used.

To:-

My Dearest Wife & Son;

I shall be home by the time this reaches you, but I thought I'd send one, they don't look too bad, it will be my first Christmas with you since 1941, so roll on that plane. Lots of love to you and Phil.

x Joxex

was utterly bewildered because I couldn't think what he looked like. I know it sounds terrible, but I couldn't. Probably the shock took the memory. It came back later. I just had to get out. I couldn't stay in the house. I went to the 'Ritz' and I saw whatever film was on but I couldn't have told you what it was when I came out. I don't think I saw any of the film really. You'd think it would have made an impression but it didn't. Everything seemed to be happening at once. My whole world seemed to fall apart.

I was an afterthought in the family. My mother was forty-three when I was born and there was a big gap between me and my sister and brothers. Long drawn out and I was the last bit. I found out that she wasn't pleased to be having me. My Mum had a sister and they were just like a jam sandwich, they went everywhere together. One couldn't bear to be apart from the other. They even lived about four houses apart. I once heard them talking and my aunt said to my Mum, 'Well, she was meant you know. I know you didn't want her but she was meant.'

They didn't know I could hear them. It went through me, I was ever so upset. 'Nobody loves me!' You know how you are when you're a kid but my aunt said 'She's sent for a purpose.' As things turned out I was because when everybody else was either dead or abroad and getting killed and my sister was here with her invalid husband there was only me that could go to work. But then, with my brother dead and Mum and Dad wrapped up in each other, I felt like a stranger, that I didn't belong and all those feelings of not being wanted came back. You know how sensitive you are at that age. Eventually it all got ironed out but it was pretty bad at the time. I just couldn't cope with seeing my mother so ill and my Dad so worried and unhappy because they'd been my rocks. That's what mothers and Dads are, aren't they?

My Mum and Dad were always very affectionate. They weren't like a lot of people, a bit stiff and stodgy. I never knew my Dad to leave the house without kissing my Mum, it was a little hug and a kiss and the same when she went out so, in the end, it was my Dad pulled her through. He did everything he could to support her.

My sister and me were like a bit of spare dropped off. She wasn't living at home so there was just me there. I was never neglected but the bond between husband and wife got them both going on to help one another and I felt left out at times. Not that there was any physical deprivation or hitting or anything like that. I just wasn't in this close circle.

I had a cousin who lived down the street and he was my twin soul shall we say. We were inseparable. It was him that supported me. When I was smaller I used to go and play with him and we used to swap comics; Rover and Wizard and all that sort of thing. We really were close. My Mum and Dad encouraged him to come here because I was on my own so I think he helped me. Him and his friends.

My Mum and Dad couldn't talk about it at the time. It was made worse because we didn't know how he'd died or where he was buried. All we knew was that he'd been sent out to Egypt and that's where he'd died. Nothing more. My Mum scoured the whole area trying to find someone who'd been with him. He'd been in a local regiment so I got the job of going round with my Mum asking if anybody had mentioned it in their letters. She was desperate to know exactly what had happened. She couldn't rest; she had to find somebody who was near him. We went everywhere in this area. I hoped that every house we went to would be able to tell us something that would give her some peace but it didn't happen. It was a fruitless search and didn't bring her any peace.

During that same week in November my Dad's brother and his family turned up at our house. They lived in Coventry and it had been so badly bombed that all they had in the world was in a few parcels and a bag. Their home had fired and they'd scrambled for a few possessions. How they'd got to here with all the train services disrupted I don't know but we took them in.

While they were with us they had word that their son had been trapped fast in a blazing tank. When he came back we didn't know him because his face was badly burned. We didn't know him until he spoke.

It seemed as if all around us there was tragedy. Mum was a big chapel-goer so she had her faith. Losing my brother shattered it a bit but she gradually got it back. It was just this terrible sense of loss. Eventually it passed. It has to pass, doesn't it?

News *was coming in all the time of casualties. Two brothers in one family lost with the Ark Royal, another two brothers lost on a Russian convoy. Several of our neighbours lost sons, many on planes which did not return to base, leaving an almost desperate hope that they had been taken prisoner.*

Many of the boys with whom we'd laughed and chatted so recently fell and were buried abroad and each one left scars and deep wounds on our lives.

"THEIR NAME LIVETH FOR EVERMORE"

ROLL OF HONOUR

HEANOR
G. APPLEBY
M. ANGELL
FRED BAKER
T. W. BARKS
A. BEER
A. BOOTH
T. F. BAMBER
S. L. BROWN
F. BENNIESTON
T. CLIFTON
J. DAVIS
N. DUNCAN
J. FROGGATT
J. GROVES
F. GOTHERIDGE
H. HARDY
A. HIBBERT
B. HIBBERT
J. HUTCHINSON
W. H. HOLMES
R. W. HOLMES
S. W. JACKSON
F. LOCKTON
H. MARTIN
C. W. MARTIN
H. MOTT
A. MAYCOCK
J. A. MOUNTFORD
L. D. OTTEWELL
A. A. PRESTON
A. PRINCE
F. PALFREYMAN
A. S. PRYOR
K. M. POWDRILL

E. SIMMS
S. SHARDLOW
T. SAXTON
L. R. SHARMAN
G. SHEPHERD
A. WEBSTER
P. WEBSTER
A. WHITE
N. YATES

LANGLEY MILL
C. ASHMORE
W. H. BAILEY
F. BAKER
NORMAN BARFIELD
G. N. BARFIELD
C. R. BESTWICK
G. S. BOLTON
ERIC BRADLEY
JOHN BRADLEY
J. BRAY
J. E. BROWN
JOHN BROWN
T. W. A. BULLIMAN
E. CHAMBERS
H. A. DARRINGTON
I. DRAPER
R P. GILBERT
T. HF.NSHAW
A. HILL
A. HITT
H. HITT
R. HITT
D. H. HOLMES
A. E. HUTCHBY

F. LONG
A. LONGDON
J. A. W. NEALE
H. PACEY
H. PAYNE
W. SEVERN
G. H. SMITH
J. SMITH
W. A. SMITH-CROSS
A. TEAGLE
G. R. WILES

MARLPOOL & LANGLEY
J. H. AUSTIN
A. AMOS
K. BALDWIN
R. BOWER
FRANK BAKER
E. BERRY
C. W. BROWN
P. E. BROWN
F. BAKER
R. J. BROWN
J. H. COOPER
J. L. COOK
A. G. DAKIN
L. EYRE
P. FLINT
D. FLINT
A. E. FOULD
H. HUTCHINSON
A. HODGKINSON
K. KRAWZYK
F. KNOWLES
A. LONGDON

J. T. MILWARD
C. W. MARTIN
A. MEE
H. MARTIN
J. E. NICHOLSON
F. STEEL
D. STALEY
J. STEED
E. SIMMS
A. STEVENS
R. WATSON
H. WALKER
J. W. WRIGHT

CODNOR
D. W. BUNTING
F. W. M. V. FOWLER
THOS. RADFORD

LOSCOE
R. S. ALLEN
A. BENNETT
W. BREWIN
D. W. BUNTING
G. BURROWS
W. CRIPPS
F. EDWARDS
G. HUTCHINSON
W. KEMP
F. MARSDEN
W. H. MOON
H. ROOME
S. TURNER
L. WILLIAMS

"THEY SHALL NOT GROW OLD, AS WE THAT ARE LEFT GROW OLD, AGE SHALL NOT WEARY THEM NOR THE YEARS CONDEMN; AT THE GOING DOWN OF THE SUN AND IN THE MORNING, WE SHALL REMEBER THEM."

3: Nice Work If You Can Get It

George Gershwin

I don't think I'd ever worked so hard in my life! Or so fast. We were well paid but believe me we earned every penny.

" It makes me laugh when they say women canít do this job or that job. We did it in the war, farming and everything. Except mines. I wouldn't go down the mines. I think the only time you go down a hole is when you're dead. "

My wife Joyce, my girl friend at the time, and her partner decided to work flat out for one shift to see how many 20mm shells they could turn out on the band-turning lathe. Ted Tickner arranged it so that the machine was given priority in supplying and taking away batches of shells. To make sure the machine was working as much as was possible breaks were arranged to cover the two girls and myself throughout the shift. I have to say that some of the other girls in the machine shop thought they were bloody mad.

At the end of the shift they had produced more than 2200 shells. That seemed an amazing amount. They checked the figures again and they were right. It brought congratulations from the head of the firm — but no extra money!

" I didn't turn my nose up at a few black-market stockings. "

There were six aluminium bars that turned in six operations. The bars were put into the machines and a nose end would be formed. The machines ran on oil to cool the operations, but sometimes the oil would catch fire and that was very frightening. I worked during the dinner hour looking after three Big Brittains. One of the machines caught fire and struggling with a very heavy fire extinguisher I managed to put it out. The setters cheered. And so they should. They were having a quiet smoke outside.

First I was a machine minder on single spindle lathes, then, when women and girls took over that job, I worked in the bar stores making sure the various machines were always supplied with bars.

Single spindle auto shop, Collaro Ltd.

Later still I trained under experienced setters and became, at the age of 17, a tool-setter on capstan lathes. I was in charge of seven lathes and when they were fully manned there were fourteen women and girls under my charge. We produced 20m/m AP shot for Oerlikon cannon. Many more things were produced there, 40 m/m Bofor shell fuses and tracer containers at the rear of the shell. The workers in 'The Pen' stamped the acceptance mark, an arrow, on bullets and shell cases.

" To go into Collaro's it was like a prison camp. "

I was very much in awe of the London folk. My immediate boss was Mr. Marsh the Company Secretary but we all had work to do for Mr. Collaro and he had a special buzzer for each secretary. Mine was four buzzes!!

Mr. Collaro sent for me one day. God, was I scared! I was shaking at the knees. He had noticed I had a flair for figures and said I must go to the Sunbrook School in Nottingham one day a week to be trained on a comptometer. He knew my parents couldn't afford to send me so he said he would foot the bill. That was when I went to the Wages Department and I stayed there. I loved going to the College and I eventually passed all the exams. It was a wonderful opportunity and I was grateful to have been able to go.

Mr. Collaro was a very smart gentleman and I'm sure he had a different suit everyday and very smart shoes. He was a ladies man and I could tell a tale or two. But I won't.

His son John was a chip off the old block and came into the office from time to time. I think he was at some University. He took me to the cinema in Nottingham, back row of course. I felt very important going out with the Director's son in a posh car but I never went again. He came on too quickly for my liking.

We all got along well, though. Even the lorry drivers who came from different parts of the country collecting scrap metal were part of it. When the foreman's wife had her baby there was a notice on the stage — on the blackboard and easel — 'Congratulations Frank on your splendid outcome!!' His wife had had twins.

One of the Londoners worked on the same shift as me. He was a proper ladies man but I never bandied words with him. We used to call him Spitz because he could always tell us when there was going to be an air-raid. He even knew when they'd started on D-Day

You had to be very precise, very exact. A fraction out and it wouldn't pass.

Mind you, there was one woman who didn't bother about precision. She was going to leave and she'd been teaching me the job on primers. She'd got the bar up on the end to make it smooth and instead of just taking a slither off she cut a piece that must have been about two inches and dropped it in the bottom of the machine. The director just happened to come up that minute and really shouted at her. 'Don't you ever do that again. Do you know that would cost four-pence?' But she wasn't bothered because she was leaving anyway.

It was a real shock. Most of us had come from light, clean airy workplaces; Aristoc where we made stockings, The Lace Factory, I & R. Morley. Now we worked in conditions that were appalling.

There was all this oil. Awful oil that smelt. It was used to cool the tools so that they didn't seize up but it went everywhere. The soles on our shoes rotted and our boiler suits were wet through with it. Worst of all it caused dermatitis. Before clocking in we used to rub our arms with anti-rash cream then tie a rag round our wrists to try to stop the oil running up our sleeves. It didn't work. I used to buy Iglodene, a watery sort of ointment, to put on it. Or we'd go along to the surgery in the factory.

The sisters who ran it — well — Ellie — she was a monkey. She'd have her bottom showing through her overalls. She never wore a support. She'd say 'You young girls shouldn't have those things on', meaning our corsets.

It got very cold at night. Cold enough to have two lots of clothing on and trousers, then sweaters and a boiler suit. While I was working on my machine I felt something hot inside my suit. I was desperate to get to the toilet and get it out but you couldn't just go and leave your machine.

Someone had to fill in for you because it was on a conveyor belt and the work would pile up if it was left. As soon as someone was free to take over I rushed to see what had happened. It was a 'Number Two' that had fallen in and burnt my skin. Not a good way to spend the rest of the shift.

The toilets were used for the odd cigarette break too. Because smokes were in short supply you could buy five at a time from the offices. Out we'd troop, across the yard and into the toilets for a quiet smoke.

Sometimes we were just so tired we didn't know how to keep our eyes open.

The pen was in darkness and after we'd been to do spot-checks on the machines we sat in Mr. Christopher's office to write our reports. I'm afraid one night we put our heads on the desk and dropped off to sleep!

The following night a note was left for us from Mr. Christopher. Someone had seen us and reported us and we'd been summoned to see Mr. Christopher, in his office, the following Monday morning. We honestly thought we would be given our marching orders but he said he realised how tiring it was and just gave us a mild telling-off. Our jobs were saved. He was a real gentleman.

I used to hate it when we were going to work on nights and it was a gorgeous, sunny night. Everybody else was going out and enjoying themselves. But then in the bad weather, and we had such bad winters then, a real distinction between summer and winter, we still had fun. One very big fall of snow left us wondering how we were going to get to work. It wasn't bothering me too much because I was only a few minutes away. I remember my mother saying to my Dad, and he was only as tall as me, 'Go down with her. Walk down the street and make a path for her and if you get lost I'll come and look for you!' I got to the bottom of North Street where Langley Mill church is and two of my friends were walking along. Our scarves were right up to our eyes because it was really biting and we made a path right down to Collaro's in the middle of the road. When we got in to clock on Vic had got newspaper up to his knees and his cap down here and Madge was killing herself with laughing.

He said 'The trouble with you is Madge, you're too fussy!'

The night after there were quite a few turned up. They'd walked from Loscoe and Ripley way. Loscoe's a mile away from here and Ripley about four. The snow was piled up a good five feet high at the side of the road.

Mr. Collaro had a big blackboard put up in the canteen and thanked everybody for coming in because otherwise we were going to hold up production. People did put themselves out because he was a very considerate boss.

Some of us had to go away to work. The factory might not have been a clean place to work but at least we were with friends. It wasn't always that way when we went to London.

I was sent, with another girl, to Woolwich Arsenal. We stayed with a Mrs. Taylor. I'll never forget her. She was absolutely awful to us. She couldn't have cared less if we were cold — and we were. It was January or February, a very bad winter with thick snow. One night we were so cold we went to a cinema in Woolwich just for some warmth. We'd put one coat over our knees, the other over our shoulders and we cuddled up in a two-seater. They were the courting seats but never mind that, there we stayed. This was the time when doodle-bugs were falling on London and the next morning we heard that the bus we should have gone back on had been bombed by a doodle-bug. That would have been it. We wouldn't have stood a chance.

Woolwich Arsenal was near the river and there were quite a lot of boat people who used to go in the canteen. We got talking to some of the seamen, telling them how awful it was and how cold we were and I think they felt sorry for us. One day they walked in and gave us both an orange!

Every factory or place of work had a 'Home Guard' unit so on top of working twelve hour shifts, six days a week, we had exercises to go to in our 'spare' time.

I used to like getting down to Collaro's. After you'd done your exercise you'd go into the canteen. Mrs. Collaro put a good feast on. Pork pies about

Wages and costing office,
Collaro Ltd. 1944.

Hand presses and second oper-
ation machines, Collaro Ltd.
1944.

The first Mrs. Collaro.

a yard square! And we had a bit of fun. When we were issued with tin helmets a couple of the lads took it into their heads to go outside and throw half-bricks in the air to test out how effective the helmets were. They both survived the experiment proving that they did offer protection at least against falling bricks. Bombs or masonry might have been a different story.

We trained with Molotov Cocktails, bottles containing inflammable liquid ignited by a piece of rag soaked in the same concoction and lit just before they were thrown. Later versions did away with the external rag and contained white phosphorous that ignited on exposure to air.

The first session with the mark two version was during daylight hours and members of the platoon working night shift went to inspect the target, a breeze block wall. It produced the eerie effect of boots walking about in the air.

A few of us volunteered to stand guard when the factory was closed for a week, the only week I can remember it not being up and running. It was two o'clock in the morning, pitch black and we heard a noise in the hedge. Rifles loaded, bayonets fixed we went very cautiously towards the noise. My partner was ahead of me on the other side of the hedge. I heard him give the usual challenge — 'Halt — who goes there?' No reply. 'Halt — who goes there?' Still no reply. 'Halt or I fire!'

'No', I shouted. 'Don't shoot!' I'd found the source of the noise. A horse having an early morning snack. We kept it quiet. If we'd told anyone we'd never have heard the last of it.

They were awful working conditions but that's only one part of the story. We had some smashing times. Don't imagine it was all doom and gloom because it wasn't. We had some fun. We had to work hard but so long as it got done no one minded you enjoying yourself. Music was a godsend to us all.

Bless 'em all, bless 'em all,
Collaro, Uretti will fall.
Bless Vladimir and Frank Morrell too,
Bless Mr. Ford he should be in the zoo,
And they're saying goodbye to us all,
And back to our benches we'll crawl,

> You'll get no enjoyment from Collaro's employment,
> So cheer up my lads bless 'em all!'

That's what we used to sing whilst we worked at our benches. Once someone started singing at one end of the factory it went right through to the other end. 'Down at the Old Nally Works' was another and 'When the Blinking War is Over.'!

There was music piped through the factory, 'Music While You Work' from the radio. Someone would start singing along with it then everyone'd join in. Over a thousand voices singing at once. The atmosphere was electric. It made you feel good inside.

I remember someone wrote a letter of song titles, all joined up together. Something like — 'Dearly Beloved',

I am 'Yours' 'Night and Day' and so on.

Have you heard of the '4 C's'? It was our own dance band formed by four Londoners. Ernie Paffey was on piano, Eddie Nickels on saxophone, someone whose name I forget played banjo and Nobby was on drums. You knew there'd be a dance when people started moving tables back. Out would come the chalk for the floor and we'd dance the night away.

When you're working twelve hours at a stretch you need good, nourishing food, especially when it was in short supply at home. Mrs. Collaro managed the canteen and put really good spreads on.

I was always ready for mashed potatoes with a sausage on top or a spoonful of mince finished off with baked beans. When you worked nights, if you were lucky, you got a break at five o'clock. That's when we tucked into thick chunks of bread and dripping and cocoa. You really had to force yourself to get it down, but you did.

I looked forward to the morning break when I could enjoy a crusty cob with a grated cheese filling. Mrs. Collaro made a delicious fruit cake and we had that in the afternoons. It was a really busy place, so many people, all on shifts, to be catered for. With everyone mixing in like that there were bound to be misunderstandings, some of them really funny. One of the London

ADULT FIRST AID

THE GRAND PRIORY IN THE BRITISH REALM OF
THE VENERABLE ORDER OF THE HOSPITAL OF ST. JOHN OF JERUSALEM
(Ambulance Department)
The St. John Ambulance Association
(One of the Red Cross Organizations of Great Britain)

Patron: HIS MAJESTY THE KING (Sovereign Head of the Order)
President: MAJOR-GENERAL H.R.H. THE DUKE OF GLOUCESTER, K.G., etc.
(Grand Prior of the Order)
Director of Ambulance and Chairman of Committee:
BRIGADIER-GENERAL SIR JOSEPH BYRNE, G.C.M.G., K.B.E., C.B.

This is to Certify that

Betty Brown

has attended a Course of Instruction at the

Langley Mill Branch of the Association,
and has qualified to render "First Aid to the Injured"

Chief Secretary

Director of
Ambulance

April 19 43

Registered at St. John's Gate, Clerkenwell, London, E.C.1

It gives me great pleasure in
handing you this certificate which I
hope will give you as much satisfaction
as I had in having you as a member of
the Home Guard.

Major
O.C.D Coy

RBNF/216/3

I have received The King's command
to express His Majesty's appreciation
of the loyal service given voluntarily
to her country in a time of grievous danger
by

BETTY BROWN

as a Woman Home Guard Auxiliary.

The War Office,
London.

Secretary of State
for War

The C.I.A. Office, Collaro Ltd.
1944.

fitters said 'Look at that 'Moggy'. Well, you'd never seen anything like it. Girls screamed and jumped on the chairs, asking where the mouse was because to us locals a 'Moggy' was a mouse. They all laughed and pointed to a cat because to them a 'Moggy' was a cat!

We had to take our breaks in turn so that the canteen staff could cope with us. Same with the tea breaks. A bell used to go and so many would go at a time. They'd come back and others would go.

We used to have four breaks besides dinner. Two before half-past-one and two in the afternoon. We were there twelve hours so we needed them, believe me.

If it was anyone's birthday we'd have a party in the canteen. We'd all bring some food and Mrs. Collaro would put on something a bit fancy. It made the day something a bit special.

" I was very envious of the other girls at break-time because they had the tastiest cheese cobs and I had a mouth full of ulcers and couldn't eat at all. "

The sirens went one dinnertime and we all had to leave the canteen. We were rushing and someone stood on my shoe and it got left behind. I hadn't got a shoe on and it was raining. So I just stood there and Frank Morell said 'Where do you think you're going?' I wasn't going anywhere, my shoe was still in the canteen!

Before the war money was really tight. We'd gone through the depression but everyone was earning such low wages. I worked a full week for eleven shillings. Collaro's changed all that. Suddenly I was earning more than my Dad and he was down the pit all day. My goodness, were our relatives jealous! We'd never been so rich.

When I got married in 1948 I was doing my time as a fitter at the Coal Board. I was getting six guineas a week for a time-served fitter and they could talk blithely about fifteen and twenty pounds. That's the comparison.

It wasn't just basic wages, either. If output increased everyone got a bonus. Every Friday afternoon Mr. Collaro would announce the bonus, thank everyone and encourage us all to keep up the good work. If the bonus was high the place rang with loud cheers. Sometimes it was as much as one hundred percent. They used to calculate the production and compare it with previous weeks. A valuation was put on it and that would be estimated out as your entitlement for the week. Time and motion you might say.

Out would come the blackboard and we'd be congratulated and shown how much production had risen by.

It helped to have friends in the wages office...

People tried really hard to do the twelve hours because of the bonus. And if you were one minute late clocking in — well — they were very strict. I just used to alter them. If it was people I knew and they were only two minutes late I used to alter it so they didn't lose a quarter of an hour.

The money soon went because our families weren't rich, We 'tipped up', gave them our wages, and they gave us our spending money back.

My Mum always said it was my wage that picked them up. It made a big difference to them. My Mum and Dad, my elder sister, a younger sister, a younger brother and a baby all lived in the one house and my Mum was able to save out of what my sister and I took home. They bought themselves a little business, top of Grace Street, when the war was finished. We had to help the war effort too, giving so much to Post War Credits that we claimed back when war was over.

I didn't save. I enjoyed having a bit more money to spend on things like stockings and make up. Not that there was much around. To make up for the shortage we used to coat our legs with wet sand, then when they were dry we rubbed it off and it left our legs stained. If I hadn't got any sand my brother would fetch it from the sand-pit on the recreation ground. I use to do them in the bath and my mum got so cross. The bath was always gritty in the

The general office, Collaro Ltd.
1944.

bottom. I'm not sure it did my eyes much good but black shoe polish was perfect for mascara.

I never spent my Collaro money. My Mum used to say all I did was sleep and work. But then I'd married during the war. Cal was away fighting and I'd never been one for going out for drinks or anything like that. Sometimes when I went to Derby station to meet Cal there'd be one or two of the girls I knew on the bus. They'd be going dancing or going to meet somebody. But honestly I never did.

I had one pound eight and six a week from the government and I lived on that. Living with Mum and Dad helped. It meant I could save the rest of my money. Of course if I wanted clothes I had to dip into it. It never went in a bank. Never. I kept it in the wardrobe in a box. There were hundreds of pounds. Six or eight hundred, something like that.

As soon as he came home, that same day, I said 'Come upstairs!' I know that sounds — but I wanted to give him this money! I made him count it. He was amazed because he couldn't save whilst he was abroad. He must have got hold of me, hugged me and all. My Mum and Dad knew I was saving it and what it was for.

They'd just started to build, this would be end of 1945, early 1946, they'd just started to build round here. They were building near where my Mum and Dad lived and we looked at one of those and they were building at Loscoe and we went up to have a look and plumped for one of those. We parted with all the money but my Mum said 'Never mind, you've got the house. You'll get something to put in it.' She lent me a bed and a wardrobe and we got a utility table, chairs and sideboard. After a while we got an easy chair and we both used to sit in that together. No stair carpet or anything. I did have a washer. But I didn't choose this washer. They just used to bring you one when you opened an account with the gas company. They sent two, one for me and one for my neighbour and she was there when they were delivered so she chose the one she wanted and I had the other. It was a boiler with a ringer and a let down top. They were marvellous really. I can't remember how much they were. I had a baby in May 1946, Tony, so I wanted a washer.

We had a garden, not a very big one but I used to grow beetroot, lettuce all that sort of thing. My Dad was a gardener, allotments and that sort of thing. I think it's passed down.

I didn't bother about paying the money out because that's what I'd saved it for. I was so proud. I can remember moving in on a Friday. They always say you shouldn't move in on a Friday. Bad luck or something. My husband had gone and taken bits and pieces from my Mum's and I pushed Tony in his pram, a lovely black, coach-built pram. Lovely. I pushed him with bits and bobs in that. It was great to go into it all new even though it was a bit bare. In those days they didn't do anything with the walls. They had to dry out for so long before you could put paper on. We didn't mind that.

It was a good start. We sold that house after eleven years, made a profit and had a big bungalow built. We were able to buy the land and my husband and my brother built it. I can remember we paid three hundred pounds for the land forty years ago and we borrowed one thousand - six hundred. It cost us two thousand six hundred pounds to build. It worked well for us.

Whatever was happening in the factory life still went on outside. We were part of it even if we didn't have much time left over.

Brenda, who came from Jersey, used to love to do our hair during tea break. One day, whilst she was messing around with someone's hair-do, she announced she and Derek were getting married. Like us they were very young. No more than eighteen or nineteen. It seemed incredible to be thinking of marriage at that age. I couldn't imagine me telling my parents that I wanted to get married. It was unheard of but I suppose when she knew Jersey had been invaded by the Germans she thought life was too short to waste.

I was courting Jack for the last two years I was at Collaro's and he used to bring me down to work the night shift. We'd go and have a drink and then he'd say 'I shouldn't go tonight,' trying to persuade me to spend the evening with him. If I didn't go in I used to get home about ten o'clock and say to my Mum 'I'm not very well so I've come home.'

" If you missed the bus coal lorries or any lorry would pull up for you. They'd open the back, up we'd hop and we'd get a lift. "

If you were married and your husband came home on leave they let you have time off but if it was your boyfriend they wouldn't.

When my boyfriend was coming home I went to the doctor and told him I couldn't eat or sleep, trying to get time off. He said 'Four hours sleep is enough for anybody.'

I got home about half-past-six one morning after working the night shift. There wasn't any chance of getting to bed though. The coal men used to tip the load on the road and it had to be brought in quickly before it was smashed by other vehicles. It was hard going. I never did get to bed that day.

" The only thing I didn't like was going out to the toilets at night. If it was foggy, and of course there's that canal right against it, you didn't know if you were going to walk into the canal or not! "

I lived with my mother-in-law whilst my husband was in the forces. Dolly, my sister-in-law, worked in the canteen. We worked together, slept together, walked to work together, so in the end it couldn't work out.

But during the air raids we used to go down the pantry and drink mother-in-law's home made wine. By the time it passed we were kaylied.

You know Lord Haw-Haw? He used to come through on radio. He lived in Macclesfield in Cheshire before he went out to Germany. One night he mentioned Collaro because the Germans had bombed us but missed. Instead they hit a bus station.

That was the night my Grandma Drew was dying and my mum was sitting up with her. It was moonlight that night. My uncle was coming up to the bungalow to check on them and the sirens had gone. There was a plane going over and he saw the bomb dropping. He dived under the hedge to

The factory and offices,
Collaro Ltd. 1944-45.

Cal Boxall

save himself.

There was a cow hit as well and ducks running round with shrapnel in their sides. It even blew my Mum's hairnet off her head.

No one was safe when the German planes were overhead. Rolls Royce workers were machine gunned as they came off the night shift at Derby but the Barrage balloons stopped many enemy planes from approaching too far inland.

There was a search light unit at Codnor that was used to search out enemy planes overhead and at Codnor Castle soldiers slept in tents, whatever the weather.

" Bombs dropped all around us. Every window from Langley Mill up towards Heanor Church on Main Road was smashed. "

Just a short time before the idea of working in such a place had seemed either terrifying or a day-dream. Now it was normal, it was what we did. And we did it well.

4: *Let's Face The Music and Dance*

Cole Porter

We worked hard but my goodness we played hard too. It was as if all the long hours, the missing our lads made us determined to get something out of life. And we did.

Jitter-bugging was all the rage and The Drill Hall was where we'd meet up with all the soldiers who were billeted in Ripley. We wanted to look as glamorous as we could to meet the fellows so getting ready to go out was a real performance.

The page-boy bob was high fashion, curled with dinky curling pins or we'd do our hair in sweeps, rolled round with hair-grips to hold it in place. Many a night I've gone to bed with my hair wet through just so that it would look right for the next day. And that was after washing it in Persil because shampoos were really hard to get. The few that were around were the powdered ones. 'Amami' setting lotion was the secret of immaculate hair according to the newspaper ads!

For the daring there was the EUGENE permanent-waving machine. We had twenty-week perm clubs that we'd organised at work, paying a shilling a week. Names were drawn out of the hat and the lucky winner ended up with curly hair. It really was a daunting experience. The machine was circular with a series of plugs and your hair was wound round a curler and then attached to an electrically heated plug. It was so heavy you'd almost be lying down before all your hair was wound and connected. Endurance was the name of the game.

All this primping didn't alter the other side of the story. It was much more difficult for us to wash our hair, no running hot water, having to dry our hair in front of the fire and, as I said, very few shampoos. 'Nits' were rife and it was quite normal to have to endure a good going over with the 'nit comb' if you had an itch on your head. It wasn't a pleasant experience because they were made of steel and almost skinned the scalp.

I'd be pursing my lips, painting on the colour and hear my Mum say 'You've got too much lipstick on!' There weren't many colours to choose from and make-up generally was hard to get hold of. Just lipsticks, powder cream in a little red tin, Palmolive vanishing cream and night cream. We put Vaseline or soot on our eyelashes to make them stand out. I cleaned my teeth

Mr. C. Collaro — Managing Director of Collaro Ltd. 1944.

with soot, too, or bicarbonate of soda.

One of the girls who worked with me used to pluck her eyebrows. We'd got a bit of spare time one night because the machine had broken down and she offered to do mine. 'All right,' I said, little knowing what I was letting myself in for. She plucked one but I wouldn't let her pluck the other. 'No way', I said. 'No way'.

We were desperate for perfumes. I've queued for hours to get 'Californian Poppy'. That was very popular. And Evening in Paris in a very small, blue bottle. If you could get that you were well away. We used to make it out of rose petals, anything, just to get something smelly.

Hats were considered THE THING! You weren't correctly dressed without one. Langley Mill had its own genius in millinery. Nellie Outram. This lady always made you feel welcome and would conjure hats of distinction with a deft twist of the wrist and a swift stitch here and there. Her well-known saying was 'Now that really suits you, love' and funnily enough it always seemed just the job. She was a much loved and respected lady.

It was heaven — heaven when I knew my Mum was going to buy me a pair of of dance shoes; my first dance shoes, gold 'T'-bar sandals with just a little Cuban heel. Two-and-eleven pence from up Heanor. I thought they were absolutely fantastic.

Frocks were a different matter. Clothes coupons meant we didn't have much of a wardrobe but if we were really stuck we'd borrow or buy from a friend. One of my friends had a lovely black georgette frock with chiffon sleeves with coloured balloons on them. I loved that dress. We were all of a size then, about seven and a half stone, so when she got fed up with it I bought it of her. My sister didn't rest until she had it off me so things were passed round about.

You needed a bit more imagination to turn an old dress into something to go dancing in but it's surprising what you can do by adding a flower or putting a lace collar and cuffs on. I had a black frock that I trimmed with sequins or a bit of fringing. A few sequins in a bow in my hair and I was ready to go.

❝ If Hitler had come back to see us having fun he'd have wanted to join us. ❞

My friend and I went dancing whenever we had the chance. We'd never miss a dance in Heanor Town Hall because that was the most likely place to get a partner, especially when our boys were on leave.

But then came the Americans, G.I's they were called, and the sailors, airmen and forces from other countries. The G.I's thought they could get anything they wanted with a bar of chocolate, chewing gum or a pair of precious stockings. All some girls were left with was a 'Bun in the Oven'!

My friend and I just flirted with anyone that could dance. We met two Air Force officers from the Royal Canadian Air Force. The one I latched on to was a Polish lad called Felix Swiezzynski. The Polish Airmen used to fall over themselves to have a dance with us. It was all great fun. There weren't that many romances though because most of the girls had already got boyfriends. I've got snapshots of me and my sister with two Navy boys and one of me with an airman. We tried them all.

That night my friend palled up with Douglas. We never knew his surname.

We had a great evening, they walked us home and we naturally thought that was that. We never saw them again. It didn't stop me having quite a bit of explaining to do to my Mum and Dad when after a few weeks a letter arrived addressed to me from this Felix — R.A.F Censored! He was a bit of a romantic and the letter included a poem. I decided it would be wiser to stick to an English boy if I was going dancing again! I've still got the letter, I read it sometimes.

❝ We smoked Woodbines, Park Drives, Kensitas, Craven 'A'. Whatever we could get. You could smoke anywhere you liked, even in a doctor's surgery. We just walked in and stubbed it out in his ashtray. ❞

I loved the Big Band sound of the forties. My favourite was Glenn Miller and 'American Patrol' with Joe Loss and 'In the Mood' a close second. There were lovely songs; 'Jealousy', 'You'll Never Know How Much I Love You',

Judy Garland singing 'The Trolley Song,' 'Coming In On A Wing And A Prayer' and 'That Lovely Weekend'. So many lovely songs.

Dancing was a way of letting our hair down. I went to Lillian Rath's to learn proper ballroom dancing; The Waltz, Quick-Step, Tango, Palais Glide, then over to the Bevan Hostel or the Pavilion at the top of Broadway to try them out. If there weren't many lads around you always had your best friend that you could dance with. We always went out with friends and watched out that the other one was safe.

We'd dance every night, even Saturday and Sunday afternoons if we could. When I first started courting seriously and we were thinking of getting married my mother said 'It'll take all your money and more besides to keep her in shoe leather'.

When we were on nights we used to all make a rule we went out one day in the week; home from work, straight to bed, get up at twelve o'clock and meet up at the Palais at Nottingham. The tea dance, something to eat then straight back from Nottingham to clock on.

Dancing after working nights had its own problems. I loved going to Alfreton, the dance was great. Trouble was when I'd been on nights I often found I couldn't keep awake.

" When we got there it was the one night there was no dance. We thumbed our way back and got a lift in a small van; two in the front with the driver and two in the back with sewing machine bits all over the floor. "

Once I took myself off to the toilet during the interval and fell asleep on the 'loo'. Thankfully someone realised the toilet door had been shut a long time. The first I knew of it was waking up to find them leaning over the top of the door and shouting to waken me up!

Another time I was short of face powder and my mother had got a lovely box of 'Coty'. Really posh. I puffed it on then realised it gave me a red, sun-burned look. Our locum doctor was at the dance that night and I'd been to see him that

week for a note off work. I really had been ill, I'd got an abscess under a tooth, but the powder made me look fit. Anyway, I just ignored him and carried on.

At the same dance I saw an old flame who was on leave from the Royal Artillery. We got talking, romance blossomed and a month after the war, on his first leave from Germany, we were married.

The cinema was a real treat. I was within a stone's throw of 'The Ritz', so I didn't have to worry about the blackout too much or catching a bus.

Those films really gave us great enjoyment. They had good stories to them and were a wonderful show. We didn't only get the film, either. Pathe News, a cartoon then the big feature. Real value for money. Wonderful.

A visit to the Odeon Cinema was special because it was so large compared to our local cinema that used to be an old chapel. That had a balcony where you had to sit sideways on. Quite a pain in the neck.

If we were on the daytime shift we didn't finish till eight in the evening so it was a mad scramble to get out. I was lucky. I could get home within ten minutes or so. Some of the others had buses and trains to catch.

Going further afield was a bit of a risk because of the air-raids and we had to carry our gas masks with us everywhere. We got a bit fed up with that. We couldn't imagine getting bombed even when we heard the bombers overhead. Mostly they were making for the bigger cities of Birmingham and Coventry but then two or three were dropped near us and fell on the fields at the top of the street where I lived. Luckily no one was hurt but after that we worried a bit more. We could have been the target that night. But we carried on — regardless!

" American Service men loved Nottingham. They always said the most beautiful girls were Nottingham girls. "

Our local postman, a Mr. Hollingworth, kept a sweet shop on High Street. It was all boarded up because of the blackout but he issued people with cards to exchange for sweets. I used to go up on Saturday night and if it was a good week I could get as many as three different kinds of sweets. There wasn't much choice but it was lovely to get some to enjoy at the pictures.

Ladding wasn't encouraged and considering we had to be home by nine o'clock sharp on working days outings weren't as sinful as we were always being told they were.

It was murder. My father was of the old school, a miner who worked nights most of the time, and he set a curfew. Woe betide anyone who wasn't in before he went to work. Whoever was out stayed out. When I was late I was grounded for a week. He was really strict. I couldn't use lipstick, powder or any kind of make up. Sometimes I used pipe cleaners to curl my hair. He didn't mind that.

A bus left Heanor Church bus stop, collecting mail at every stop along the way. Many a time I was too interested in the boys to be there on time and to see it setting off with no hope of catching it was a disaster. I'd gallop and gasp my way down the hill after it, always just a little way behind but not enough to cause disruption at home by being too late.

We spent a lot of time at the library. Going in to change our books was a perfect excuse to chat the boys on Heanor market place. That's where the Monkey Walk was. We'd walk round and round and the fellas would stand in shop doorways watching us. If they saw a girl they fancied they'd pull 'em in and we'd just stand talking. I was fourteen, young and innocent and I stopped and listened! A kiss and cuddle, that's about all it was. It was all innocent and above board.

" On a Saturday morning all of us used to go to work with our turbans on our heads because we'd got our curling pins in ready for going to the dance at night. "

A friend of mine worked on the telephone exchange and she told us to be at the phone box for a certain time and she'd talk to us. If she had a call coming in she'd have to switch off or it might be that her boyfriend, who used to sing

to her, had called. When the call came she rang us back and said 'It's my boyfriend' and we listened in. Then she said to him 'Just a minute I've got a call coming in.' and she came back to us and asked if any of could sing. My friend said I could so there I was singing to her boyfriend and he was thinking it was her!

A bit later on they started having shows at the mushroom farm where he worked. Someone must have blabbed because I had a letter from them asking me to go and audition. After that I went down and sang once a fortnight. The first Sunday rehearsal we stood having tea with all the Bevan Boys. It was lovely. Three girls and all those Bevan Boys.

> **" Happiness was dancing at Donelly and Kent's class on Derby Road, Heanor. Blissful nights were spent here. There was many a kiss and cuddle session during the intervals round the back of the dance hall! "**

A young girl had come down from Scotland to stay with us for a while. One night we went out to Ripley but when it came to catching the bus home I couldn't find her anywhere. So I went home alone and my Dad says 'Where's Annie?' He made me walk back to Ripley. My sister came with me and we got as far as Codnor only to find Annie walking back with this lad. My sister told her off, not me. 'It's not your fault,' she said to me because I was really upset. If you had to walk home there was always some boy who'd walk with you in all innocence.

I suppose we valued our leisure time because it was so limited, having a few hours here and there. The night shifts were the worst when our days were taken up with sleeping, especially in the winter when the days were short.

It was dark by tea-time and you certainly didn't get much fresh air. My mother got quite concerned if I slept too long, but sleep you did. It was very exhausting work on those big machines. No wonder there was no need to go on diets. The exercise kept you slim. But we did find time somehow to do the things we wanted to do. My main pastime was music, the church choir and a mixed choir. They were the means of people getting together and having a time of relaxation.

Days out were a real treat. My sister was courting a soldier who was stationed at Stoke-on-Trent and myself, my sister and my boyfriend dressed up and went to see him. My sister and I were as pleased as punch with our new shoes.

He was stationed in this big house and, of course, sugar was rationed, and he got us some. Not just a bit. He filled a shopping bag with it. We caught a train back from Stoke-on-Trent to Derby, missed the last bus to Heanor and had to walk. We walked and walked and I thought we were nearly home but we were only at Chester Green. My shoes were beginning to hurt me. I took a smaller size than my sister so we changed over. She squeezed into my mine and I flopped about in hers.

There used to be all these stone outpost things, there was one on Breadsall Hill, with a sentry. We daren't go by because we'd got this sugar. If he wanted to know what was in the bag we'd have been in trouble. We absolutely crept by, we were terrified. It was a bright moonlight night and when the sirens went Cal said 'They'll see us on this road' and made us lie in the ditch. Well — we'd got lovely new navy blue coats — you can imagine what they looked like. When we got to where Broomfield College is we caught up with a chap.

'Can I help you carry your bag?' he asked but we didn't dare let him in case he wanted to know what was in it!

My Mum was frantic when we got home because it was so late. There she was hanging out of the bedroom window. I can't remember what she said about the sugar — I expect we used it — but it was funny.

If we weren't out on the town there was always plenty to do at home.

We had our jobs to do. Not my younger sister, she was too small, but my elder sister and me. Whoever did the front room did the passage from the front door to the living room door. Whoever did the kitchen had the pots to wash all week and do the brasses and cutlery. That was on a Saturday morning.

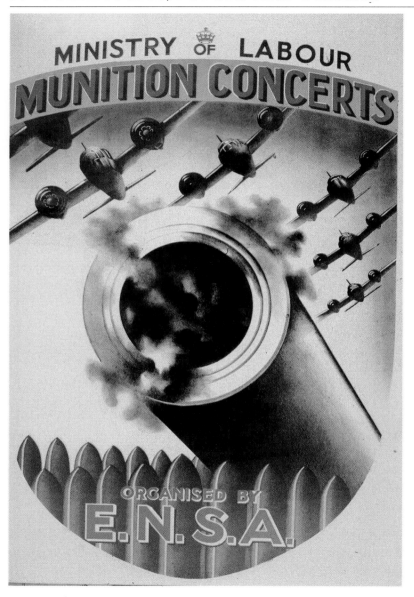

We'd got a large attic that covered the whole house and was up four flights of stairs. It had a wooden floor and once every three weeks or so my sister and me had to get a bucket, a scrubbing brush, soft soap and clothes and cart them up all the way up the stairs. She'd start at one end and I'd start at the other. Then we'd have to go down to empty our buckets. You can't wash a floor with dirty water. Then up the stairs again.

Monday night was a 'stay-in' night for me because it was washday. After Mum had done the washing for six of us my eldest sister and I had to do all the ironing while Mum went off to do her Red Cross duties at Heanor Hospital. We only had one gas iron and two flat irons. I hated it when it was my turn to use the flat irons on half the kitchen table.

We'd have the battery radio on for 'Monday Night at Eight O'Clock' and it made it seem as if the ironing was easier.

Another night would be bath and hair washing night.

On the nights when we'd got time to sit down we wrote letters to our boyfriends or played card games, dominos, darts. It was just so good to relax.

My mother wasn't a strong person and as I lived with them I was head cook and bottle-washer. There were eight others at home so it was work at home and at work. The only spare time I had was if my husband came home on leave. Then it was a round of visiting. On one particular leave we went to my mother's sister at Corkley. Her son was on his embarkation leave before going to North Africa. I shall never forget my husband and my cousin embracing one another and wishing one another luck. But shortly after wards we heard he was missing believed killed.

***K**ath and I went to school together and were true friends. When I was fifteen, sixteen, I'd take Albert's letters round and read them to her. She and Albert were good friends and she'd introduced me to him.*

She'd lost her brother in the war and we supported one another through that and went together to the Armistice service at Langley Mill Church. They were really traumatic times. The church would be absolutely packed and the band would come up from Langley Mill with the British Legion flag. It makes me go cold when I think about it. Bill Tame led them, he was a big figure in the British Legion, and they'd all march into church. They made the rafters ring, you know.

The 'Roll of Honour' was on a screen at the front of the church and they'd read every name out. There was never a dry eye in the place. We remembered all the boys of Langley Mill, not just Kath's brother, because there were two or three out of my street that got killed. Boys we'd grown up with, only as old as us. It was a very sad time.

Strange really. We'd dance, sing, watch films, get on with living. And all the time we'd remember. I suppose it's always been the same.

5: *When The Lights Go On Again All Over The World*

Seller, Marcus and Benjamin

'This is the B.B.C. London on the 6th. June 1944.

Earlier today Allied troops landed in Normandy and several beachheads have been secured on wide fronts. The invasion of Europe has begun, taking war to the enemy.'

" On D-Day I was cycling past Codnor Castle on my way to work and the sky seemed full of aeroplanes. Later in the morning all the machines were turned off and it was announced that our lads had landed in Normandy. "

The words may not be exact but that's what they meant.

We were coming to the end of a night shift when, suddenly and totally unexpectedly, the power was cut off. We gazed at each other in bewilderment as the noise from the machines died away into an eerie silence and lights flickered to emergency power. The radio crackled through the tannoy system bringing its stark message. There was no cheering, no hurrahs. We just took in the news and all it implied. Our thoughts were with the troops and the dangers they were exposed to. Men and women alike hugged each other and many silent prayers were offered up for their safety and protection.

In the raw emotion of the moment tears were shed quite openly by both men and women.

It was the culmination of a year of preparations. Intense Air Force bombings and airborne troops had begun the work. The flotillas of small ships and boats loaded with soldiers had waited for the signal that would move us towards peace. But it was to be another ten months before we would celebrate V.E. Day; months when the first V-1 flying bombs hit Britain, followed by 1000 V-2 rockets that fell on London, killing nearly three thousand people and injuring many more.

A matter of days after Hitler's suicide Germany surrendered and on May 8th. 1945 we celebrated Victory in Europe.

Multi spindle auto shop, Collaro Ltd.

You could have heard a pin drop. All the machines were shut down, all work stopped. The news came over the tannoy and a huge cheer went up. Not much work was done for the rest of the day! I felt terribly sorry for a girl I worked with. For the rest of us there was so much relief, such a feeling of happiness that our boyfriends and husbands would be coming home. Some were crying tears of joy. But for this young girl it was very different. Her husband had been killed in the Navy and she was heartbroken; they hadn't been married long and he was so young.

My Mum and Dad were so relieved and excited because my brother was in the 8th. Army and had been in the thick of the fighting in Italy. It was like a huge weight being taken off us. We seemed to be floating.

Everyone wanted to celebrate in any way they could. At Eastwood they painted a huge Union Jack on the ground and had balloons and flags everywhere.

At Argyle Street, Langley Mill we formed a committee to organise a street party. A few other streets were with us; Bank Street, Gladstone Street, Campbell and Queen Street. In the end the weather spoiled it for us and the 'street' party was held in the Chapel at the bottom of Argyle Street. All the children and neighbours came, danced, sang, had a lot of fun. There were Union Jack's flying everywhere and Heanor Market Place was packed with people. We danced in the Market Place! I remember my brother and me 'Doing the Lambeth Walk — Oi!'.

That night myself, my sister and a young auntie of mine went for a walk round Shipley. None of us had ever been in a public house on our own before but we just had to celebrate so we braved it and went in the 'Brick and Tile' for a sherry. We were so happy.

The people who were at work at Collaro's that night had their own celebration that didn't have the happy ending they'd all imagined.

We decided to have a bonfire on the ground between the factory and the canal. The wood was piled so high. It was going to be a magnificent show during our evening break. Paddy Leary, one of the mechanics who came up with the firm from London, tried to make a firework. I'm not sure what went wrong but it exploded whilst he was working on it and he lost some fingers. A sad end to our joy that the war was over.

The war really was over.

All over the country crowds gathered in impromptu celebrations and for the first time in six years the street lights were switched on all over Britain.

But we still had to wait for the war with Japan to finish. On the 15th. August, 1945 the Japanese surrendered. Over a million people crammed into Times Square in New York. Sydney's streets were showered with ticker-tape thrown by office workers and crowds surged onto the lawn of the White House. Everyone had their own way of celebrating peace.

My husband was on leave and, as a treat, we'd booked to go on a day trip round Derbyshire. Then came the news of the surrender of the Japanese. That day out was a real celebration. We enjoyed it so much especially knowing that very soon we wouldn't be parted again and could get on with our life together.

Some friends of ours and their little son were on holiday in Skegness. Things were just opening up again. The Pleasure Beach was up and running but the music on the roundabouts was still pre-war. 'Sister Susie's Sewing Shirts for Soldiers' was played over and over again. The barbed wire defences were still on the beaches and the concrete lookout posts were still in position but it didn't stop everyone running out and dancing round and round the trees. Such happiness.

Even before VJ day some servicemen and women had begun to return home.

It was a never-to-be-forgotten time for me. My husband came home from India in June 1945. I hadn't seen him since we'd married in 1942 and then we'd only had two days together before he went away.

I met his train at Derby railway station and I can't begin to describe my feelings. They were wonderful, that I know and the moment when we met for the first time in three years will live with me forever.

My cousin Madge was pregnant when her husband went abroad. He was away nearly five years and when he returned home Megan, his child, wouldn't have anything to do with him. She screamed and screamed. It took weeks before she would kiss him or let him nurse her.

Some soldiers never had that chance.

Before he went abroad my cousin's wife had a baby girl. He saw her once, the day she was born, and was killed a few months later. Sandra, his daughter, never knew her daddy.

Strange how it works out. Another cousin went through the war from the start to the end without a scratch and is now eighty-two years old.

" My husband was on his way to work when someone asked him where he was going. When he told them they said 'You fool — don't you know it's all over?' "

We held homecoming parties for our boys as they were de-mobbed and repatriated. There always seemed to be one going on somewhere. Some of the less fortunate had to be transferred from Army hospitals to our own civilian hospitals to recuperate from their injuries. Many of them had suffered terrible injuries. Even the lucky ones took time to come to terms with civilian life again. And so did we.

Peace brought other changes as life gradually got back to normal.

Some things changed almost immediately, others took longer. Factories began to make peace time articles; stockings, underwear and such like but rationing was still in force. It was years before you could buy furniture without dockets. Blackouts were pulled down, street-lights restored and buses and cars were able to run with their lights full on. Gas masks were thrown out or put in lofts 'just in case'. Where there'd been vegetable plots we began to see lawns and gardens. But it all took time.

As soldiers were returning and life began to get back to normal other people were getting ready to leave. Collaro's important role in the war effort had come to an end and many of the people who'd come to Langley Mill from London now returned to try to pick up their lives. Once again Aristoc and The Lace Factory would employ the people who'd left them to work at Collaro's. But not everyone went back to their old jobs.

"My husband had come home on leave just a fortnight before my baby was born. She was eleven months old before he saw her again. "

It was a sad day when the firm moved back to Peckham. For some time the friends we'd worked with and really got to know had talked of getting home again. I had the chance to go with them because Mr. Collaro wanted all our family to go back with them. He was going to buy us a house but we decided we wanted to stay in Derbyshire. People gradually said their goodbyes and there were many tears shed. The ones who were left behind began to think about new jobs.

I'd worked in the wages office at Collaro's and didn't want to go back to shop work. Instead I went to Eastwood Hall working for Major Barber who owned all the collieries in that area. Eventually they were taken over by the Government and then became The National Coal Board.

It was a good place to work but I must admit I really missed all my friends and the atmosphere at Collaro's. I kept in touch with my close friends.

The mining industry was ever so lax. We used to get the money from the bank, check that we'd got the right amount, then take it round to the different coal yards. There was no one to take care of us so we used to sit on the money to hide it. We used to make the money up, great piles of it, with no security. It went into little tin cans and each one had a number. The men just came to the window, passed a disc over and were paid according to the

The second Mrs. Collaro.

number on the tin. They'd have got their pay slip beforehand so that they could see they were going to be paid the right amount before they collected their wages. After working somewhere where security was top priority it took some getting used to.

Not everybody found their new work lived up to expectations, especially after the type of work they'd been doing.

I did all sorts. I couldn't seem to settle. Aristocs then Raleigh's, then a cosmetics firm. I even worked with an aunt who was a hairdresser but this was without a wage because I was being taught how to perm with the new Langford perms. Not bringing in money wasn't any good to my mother so I moved on.

Even in Nottingham I wasn't earning enough to cover the cost of the train journey; a pass was twelve and six pence a month.

Eventually I went along to the Labour Exchange and asked if I could have a green card to find out what was on offer. The lady on the desk offered me a job on the buses. Well, I didn't fancy that so I said 'That won't do. I'm no good at reckoning'.

She got quite nasty and said they'd have to stop my dole.

I said 'Hold on a minute. I haven't had any yet!'

Eventually I went to Players in the leaf room and worked there for three or four years.

It was horrible. A different atmosphere entirely. At Collaro's you had a freedom, as long as you did your work. You could sing your head off, do what you liked. And you could go to the toilet when you wanted, within reason. There were no sort of ties. But at Morley's you'd gone from a big factory into a small factory, into a confined space with about twenty, twenty-five people to a room. No music piped in and if you talked or sang to yourself you were told 'Be quiet, you're here to work.' It was worse than being at school.

Thing was, I'd gone to Collaro's straight from school so I'd never known anything different. Collaro's ran the way it did because they knew they'd get more work done if everyone was happy. Private enterprise didn't bother

Daily Mirror

MAY 2

Wednesday, May 2, 1945
No. 12,906   ONE PENNY
Registered at G.P.O. as a Newspaper.

U-Boat chief claims he's new Fuehrer, tells Huns to fight on

HITLER DEAD

"Fell at his post in battle of Berlin," says Nazi radio

Adolf Hitler, leader of the Nazi Reich since January 30, 1933, the world's chief criminal, now dead at the age of fifty-six. His career appears on Pages 4 and 5.

HITLER is dead. He "fell for Germany" in the Reich Chancellery in Berlin yesterday afternoon, according to a broadcast from Hamburg at 10.30 last night.

Grand-Admiral Doenitz, 54-year-old inventor of U-Boat pack tactics, broadcast, claiming that Hitler had appointed him Fuehrer and Commander-in-Chief of the German Forces.

Doenitz came to the microphone and declared: "The military struggle continues with the aim of saving the German people from Bolshevism.

'We shall continue to defend ourselves against the Anglo-Americans just as long as they impede our aim.''

A ghost voice broke in: " Rise against Doenitz. The struggle is not worth while if crime wins."

The new "Fuehrer" for how long?

Admiral Doenitz

Doenitz lived here —in an asylum !

WHEN 54-year-old Admiral Karl Doenitz, Germany's new Fuehrer, invented the U-boat pack, his order to crews was: "Sink without mercy."

He left his job as U-boat chief to become C.-in-C. of the German Navy in February, 1943, and his technical brilliance was always a more formidable weapon than Hitler's intuition.

The German Navy will fight to a finish," he has boasted.

During the last war he spent a considerable time in England—as a prisoner of war in a Manchester lunatic asylum.

The British sloop Snap Dragon fished him out of the Mediterranean after sinking his U-boat in 1917.

By feigning insanity after his capture he qualified for a place among the first batch of prisoners to be repatriated to Germany.

He has shown himself capable of bluntly admitting the worst and fighting tenaciously in spite of it. Admitting in 1943 that U-boats had almost domed the deep Atlantic for attacks off the American coast, he declared:

"Operating in American waters is no easy matter."

The announcement of Hitler's death at fifty-six, after being Fuehrer since January 30, 1933, was preceded by slow Wagnerian music and finally by a roll of drums.

During the announcement and Doenitz's speech from Hamburg, the southern German radio network went on broadcasting light music.

It was not until half an hour later that it put

Continued on Back Page

MYSTERY OF HIMMLER PUZZLES THE CABINET

By BILL GREIG

THE unexpected appearance of Admiral Doenitz as Fuehrer came as a shock to members of the Cabinet who have been in touch with the surrender discussions at all stages.

It had been assumed that Himmler would automatically succeed Hitler, and that this would be followed by complete surrender. What has gone wrong is not yet clear, but the belief is expressed officially that nothing has happened likely to long l255 the war appreciably.

The unknown factor is still Himmler. There are two possibilities.

That fanatical Nazis—of whom Doenitz is a fair specimen and one of the toughest —have seized Himmler to prevent surrender.

That Doenitz, as leader, is nothing more than a screen behind which still another attempt to negotiate will be

made with Himmler holding the real power.

The possibility of Himmler also being dead was now strongly rumoured some support last night, and the Government not making anxious attempts to find out the truth through neutral sources.

Despite his fighting speech, Doenitz is not considered as really intending to stage a "fight to the last man" campaign. It is felt that behind his words lies no more than a desire to hearten the German people while he makes another effort . . . behind to be in vain . . . to get terms from the United Nations.

Doenitz and his friends may have believed that Himmler had succeeded in making a deal safeguarding himself with

Britain and America. Regarding themselves double-crossed, they turned the tables on him.

That Himmler tried to save his own skin is now admitted.

It can now be revealed that it was Himmler and not Hitler who carried through all the arrangements regarding prisoners of war. He then gave the impression of being the real if not the titular head of Germany. At no time did Doenitz appear on the scene.

The possibility of Doenitz making some last desperate effort to hearten the Germans while he tries to negotiate is not overlooked here.

This might, even include a renewal of air attacks on this country, but they could only be on a small scale.

The fact that the evacuation

of Norway and Denmark had apparently begun before Doenitz spoke suggests that Himmler had actually given some orders regarding surrender earlier in the day.

Attention is drawn to the fact that, although Doenitz tried to suggest that Hitler died in action he carefully avoided saying so in as many words.

From facts known in London it is certain that Hitler did not die so nobly, though his end may have been equally dramatic and not exactly from natural causes.

From one in close touch with the Government I was given this summing-up last night: "Whatever has happened in Germany last night has lengthened the war by more than a week. The military position is as clear as that. Doenitz has no navy, no organised army and only the skeleton of an air force."

about that sort of thing. All they were interested in was the money.

We'd decided that if we could find a job 'in service' we'd take it so that we'd have a roof over our heads. The gentry were very much reduced in status but we were very lucky to have an aristocrat of a boss and ended up with a lovely home at 'Lodge House'. I was the housekeeper and my husband was caretaker of fifteen acres, mostly woodland.

Even the Gentry had a price ring of set wages that were based on agricultural wages. They gave nothing away even though he was a millionaire.

But it wasn't always easy. My husband had been away fighting, I'd been working hard at Collaro's earning good money and doing important work. It was difficult to adjust to being told exactly what to do.

Here's an instant that happened. My husband used to lift the dumb waiter out of the cupboard which held the cruet, toast rack, milk and such like. Anyhow the lady of the house kept taking the top off the cruet and my husband kept screwing it back. I knew nothing about this but one morning at breakfast she called me back, trying to humiliate me in front of her husband. She said 'When I take the top off the cruet it means it needs filling'. Well — I saw red and said 'Oh, poor you. If it's too much of an effort for you to fill it it's time we left,' and we did. That was the end of our life in service.

*B*ut others fitted in well at their old firms.

Funny, it was as if I hadn't been away. The machines and everything seemed just as I remembered them. I had to do a few bars 'running on', that was putting the legs onto bars or needles, to show I could do it. I hadn't forgotten at all. I found it was just as easy as before. I know I was a little slower but I was pleased that after a five year rest I'd come back and almost surpassed myself. I was soon on the top ratings and joined a team of 'runners on' that I remembered from my first time there.

The housing shortage was a problem for everyone. Women who'd married during the war had often lived with their parents. Now they needed to find homes of their own.

My Mum had to have the family all back. Mum, Dad, my younger sister Meryl, Ken, his wife and daughter, myself and husband Charles all made our home together. What a happy family. It worked very well but we were a bit too crowded. Just imagine — we were never a lonely family!

It took a long while to find homes to call our own. With my brother having a little daughter and his wife having lived in Ripley they soon had the chance of a Council flat. But Charles and I were not so lucky. Every time I went to ask at the Council Offices if we were high enough on the list they kept saying 'No. You haven't any children. They count for housing.' So till then we had to stay with Mum and Dad. Seven years later we finally heard of a cottage going but we had to buy the adjoining cottage too. Then we were able to set up a home of our own. It was just a small terraced cottage where we thought we'd stay until things improved. But we stayed. And stayed. I couldn't think of leaving.

> **" You could get small oranges called 'Jesus Candles'. To this day I don't know why they were called that. "**

*W**hat a change there'd been. I'd started out as a young teenager, worked through the war in a job I could never have imagined having, and when it was all over there was the future to look forward to. A whole new world just waiting.*

The most important part of our new world was getting together with husbands and sweethearts after absences that had lasted years. For most of us our courtships had been carried out through letters. That's how we'd got to know each other. Yet we'd changed so much. Those of us who'd stayed behind had grown up, done important work, learned to be independent. The ones who'd gone away had seen far more of the horrors of war than we had and what they'd seen had changed them. They would never be able to forget.

Now it was time to make our own lives. But before we could plan weddings there was the awful job of asking our parents if we could marry.

It seems strange when everyone had been through a war to be asking permission like children. But that's how it was.

Albert and me — well — that's a story. We'd been boyfriend and girlfriend but nothing serious. I was very young and he was four years older than me. I wrote to him, that's all. By the time he was going abroad I was eighteen and it was me that broke it off. It was all a bit of a muddle. First of all I'd gone to the wrong station. We'd gone out on the Saturday night to the Ritz Cinema and he was leaving on the Monday. I told him I'd see him off and I waited and waited at Langley Mill Station but he didn't turn up. I found out he'd gone from Nottingham. Anyway I didn't write to him for one reason. There was I at eighteen and my Mum was having another baby. I was so ashamed. I felt there was a terrible stigma to it. Sounds silly now but that's how I felt. I never forgot him though. I thought about him a lot, even when I knew he was going out with a W.A.A.F.

It was strange how we got back together. He was writing to a girl whose mother worked at Collaro's and she knew Albert and I had been close. 'Write to him,' she said.

'Oh no I'm not,' I thought.

Then one of the girls started on. 'Why don't you get in touch.'

I wanted to but didn't know how to do it until it came to my twenty-first birthday party. We used to cut the birthday cake up into little pieces, like they do for weddings, and send them out to people who couldn't get to the celebration. I did that. I didn't say who it was from, I just put 'From a Sincere Friend on her Twenty-First Birthday.'

Three or four days later I got a letter back. He knew who'd sent it and wanted me to write to him.

In the meantime the mother of the girl he'd been going out with told us her daughter was getting married. Well — I thought it was to Albert because there'd been such a gap between us, so I said 'Oh, very nice' but my heart nearly stopped beating. She looked at me and said 'Don't get worried Doris. She's marrying a fellow from the R.A.F.' Once she'd gone away all the girls started saying I should write to him. Really pushing me. All I could think was that he wasn't going to get me on the rebound! One night Albert's sister was waiting for me when I came off nights. 'Albert wants you to write to him.'

So I did. I wrote about ordinary things, what was happening in the village, hoping he was all right because he was in Malta and they were literally getting starved out. The ships were being bombed in the harbour.

The first letter he wrote back was nine pages long telling me how much he'd missed me and could we get back together again.

That was it. That was the second start. And it moved from 'Dear' to 'Darling' I suppose and for three years we were writing continuously. He couldn't write too much because of the censorship but now and again I'd get a 'green' letter that they didn't censor so much. It went from strength to strength.

We were very loyal to each other. There was no saying 'Oh well, he's away, I can do what I like.' It wasn't like that. If you had a boyfriend you didn't go off with others. That's how it was.

It was brilliant when he came home. He wrote to me in March 1944 from a ship that was bringing him back. I've still got that letter. I treasure it.

It was a wonderful homecoming. Brilliant.

I hadn't been sure exactly when he'd arrive but his sister let me know so I made my way to their house. They lived down an entry and as I walked up it my heart began to thud. I hadn't seen him for four-and-a-half years and suddenly I just couldn't do it. Couldn't walk in there and act naturally. I got to the back door, the living room window was on my right, and I could just see him combing his hair. 'I can't meet him. I can't,' I thought and rushed back up the entry. I was in a real state but his sister came after me.

'Come on Doris, you must come in.'

He wrapped his arms around me, said 'It's great to see you' and I just said 'Welcome Home'. That's all. His mum was crying, everybody was crying but it was so lovely to see him.

They were wonderful days, getting to know one another again and I think we appreciated one another more because of being separated for so long. He'd come home on leave and whatever shift I was on he'd come down and walk me to work or meet me at dinner-time just so that we could have an hour together. It was great because after four-and-a-half years of just writing

"Are we good? I ask you, how the blazes could we be otherwise in all this clobber?"

to each other it was lovely to think he was standing at the end of the road waiting for me.

One time some friends and I had been to the Rex cinema at Eastwood to see the 'Desert Song'. We were on our way home at the bit where there's an island now, but then we used to go straight over the canal. It dipped a bit so we were out of a sight for a little way. There we were, arm in arm, singing 'My Desert is Waiting'. I didn't realise Albert was on the other side of the canal bridge. I nearly died when I saw him. All he said was 'Your Desert IS waiting!'

Later in the year his mother had gone into hospital and we'd gone to Nottingham to see her. He was pushing me in front of jewellers windows and saying 'Is there anything you want?'

'No,' I kept saying. 'I'm not much of a jewellery person'.

When he went back off leave he wrote to me.

'I am a fool! I wanted to ask you to get engaged. Didn't you realise what I was doing?'

I hadn't.

His next leave we discussed getting married but I didn't know how we were going to tell my parents, or rather ask them.

'We'll do it together,' he said.

When we did get around to asking it was traumatic. We really were bothered what our parents would say. We wanted their approval, we always did.

I don't know if my Dad was very pleased because the Forces, at the back of our parents' minds, were people to be reckoned with.

Bless him, Albert smoked a bit then and he lit this cigarette up and broke the matchstick into a thousand pieces in his hand.

I thought 'My Dad's going to say no. He's going to say no.'

Of course he didn't. He had to relax the rules a bit. I was nearly twenty-three, not a child.

'Well,' he said, 'we expected it. But how long?'

'Not till next year.'

That was all right.

We'd got everything arranged for the wedding and then Albert nearly missed it. He'd called on his friend Doug in Wales and they'd nipped into a pub to have a drink. Whilst he was there this fellow was singing 'The Holy City' and Albert had always loved that song.

When he came out of the pub the last bus was just going down the street. He ran, took a flying leap and missed the rail. It dragged him along a bit but if he hadn't made a grab for it he'd have missed the train and wouldn't have been home in time.

We'd booked the Parish Rooms at St. Andrew's, Langley Mill for the Reception and, believe it or not, the most difficult thing was to get the food together. But everybody was great, they gave us tins of this or that, jellies, all sorts. My dad was a very good cook and he made our wedding cake. War or no war it was a four-tier one. Gorgeous. Albert took the top tier back with him for the boys.

I wore a white dress in a type of crepe with a silver thread running through it.

So there we were, married on the Saturday, up to his mother's for dinner on the Sunday and he went back on Monday, the day Hitler committed suicide. What a lovely wedding present.

" I remember my brother trying to eat a banana with the skin still on. "

One of my first thoughts was 'Oh, I daren't ask my Mum and Dad!'

I can see us now, sitting in my Mum's living room with me on his knee. We talked and talked about it. How would we ask them? What would we say?

'You ask,' he said.

So — I went into my Mum's bedroom the following morning and said it, just like that.

'Cal wants us to get married.'

'Oh, you're too young. You're too young,' she said. I was about twenty and we'd been courting three-and-a-half years. 'Anyway, you'd better see what your Dad says.'

She must have talked to my Dad and luckily he agreed.

We decided to get married in the August and made all the preparations,

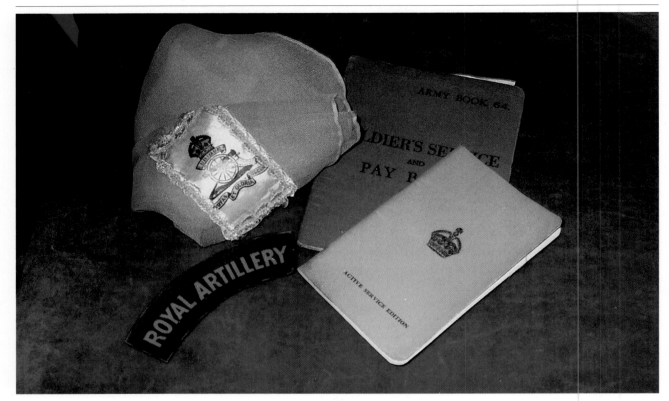

Cal and Kath Boxall nee Eley.

put the banns in. At the end of June I had a letter to say he was getting four days embarkation leave so all our plans had to be scrapped. There was no way we could know how long he'd be abroad. It was so sad. He came home on the Sunday night and we decided to go ahead, do a rush. We'd no idea how to go about it so we dashed up to Heanor Vicarage to ask Mr. Smith, the vicar, what we should do. The poor man was in bed and we'd woken him up. He was ever so nice about it.

We needed a special licence so Cal went for that the following day and in the afternoon we traipsed round looking for a wedding ring. We'd got our hearts set on a twenty-two carat gold one but couldn't find one in Ripley or Ilkeston. In the end we had to settle for something different. Even though it cost two guineas it wasn't just what we wanted. Cal put it on my finger that afternoon and said 'When things have settled I'll buy you another one, a better one.'

I didn't want a better one, I wanted the one he'd put on my finger. I said 'I don't want another, it wouldn't mean the same.'

There was no time for getting the full white wedding bit so I had a dusky pink dress and accessories. My mother put a tea on at home and we had a gorgeous cake. My Mum had been up to the Co-op at the top of Midland Road and asked the manager if he could do anything for us.

'Yes, I can, but it'll be a chocolate cake — chocolate covered.'

And it was beautiful!

We married on Tuesday and he went away Thursday morning. I didn't go to see him off, only to Derby because we didn't go far in those days, well — I didn't. I can remember walking up Stores Road from Derby station, — and the tears. I came back home to Mum. Those feelings stay in your mind forever.

It was three years before I saw him again. Then we got it wrong. He docked at Liverpool and I went to Derby! I'd said 'Let me know, send a telegram. I don't want you coming here, you must wait for me at Derby station.' I got the telegram this certain morning and went up to the Red Lion Square to catch the bus to go and meet him. Instead I missed it and had to go round to the garage and ask Frank Bowen if he'd take me to Derby in one of his cars. It cost me ten shillings but it was worth every penny.

Cal was stood there waiting and the feeling was — unbelievable. Something I'll never forget.

When we'd married and he'd had to go back after three days I didn't really feel married. I didn't have chance. When he came home it was the real beginning of our married life.

> **" My Mum's first words were 'Oh! A sugar-daddy!' because he was twenty-two, a lot older than me. But I didn't take any notice of her. "**

We'd been girlfriend and boyfriend during the war, but mostly by letter. I'd met him through a friend and when he was going into the Royal Air Force he asked if I'd write to him. That was it.

I was so excited when I knew he was coming home. It was around my birthday and I was expecting him to come home just before Christmas. I kept waiting and waiting right through Christmas and I kept thinking 'Am I going to get a telegram or letter?'

They landed in England at the end of December and it was a week or so before he got home. We didn't have a party, nothing like that. We just met up.

We were so shy. He'd been away four years and I was a very young teenager when he went away and nineteen when he came home. I'd grown up a lot from what he could remember.

He was home on leave for a fortnight and we saw each other every night. One day I said 'I'll have to stay in tomorrow. I've got to wash my hair,' and he said 'What am I going to do?' He hadn't got a clue what he was going to do if I wasn't there!

He hated his de-mob suit, absolutely hated it, and he was determined that as soon as he could have another he would. He went and got measured for this suit and in those days you had to wait six months because of the shortage of materials and man-power. He wanted it made-to-measure and tailored. During that six months we decided we were going to get married and when he got this suit I said to him 'You can't wear that now! You've got to keep it for when we get married because you can't get another.' He wasn't very pleased about that!

I stuck to my guns and I wouldn't let him wear it.

Just after we got engaged I went to see Kath who was in bed poorly and told her we were marrying.

'What about a dress?' she asked. She'd married before me. 'What about mine?' she said. I tried it on and it fitted perfectly. I borrowed the veil and head-dress from two different friends and that was my wedding outfit. Kath did my hair for me the morning of the wedding.

Once I knew Bill was coming home I'd decided I was going to pay board. My Mum wanted to know why. I said I wanted a week off to be with Bill and it wasn't fair if I couldn't pay her. She said I could still have the week off but I thought I'd got to start some time and it meant I had some money to save for our home. We had a long wait. We didn't get it for seven years. Our married life began at Mum and Dad's because council houses weren't so easy to come by. They were only just starting to build again.

We'd got our daughter before we moved out. Unless you'd got children you didn't stand a chance. You'd got to be overcrowded so once I knew my brother was coming out of the Army I pleaded with the council.

It hadn't been easy, not for any of us, not for Bill. Things weren't so bad while I was at work but once I'd had my baby and was at home Mum and I began to get on each other's nerves. I was a lot stronger character than my Mum and she didn't like it.

Soldiers returning from war meant a lot of things, but high on the list was 'Romance'. The girls who'd been too young to have boyfriends in the Forces soon fell in love with young men who were hardly out of uniform.

Funny how things work out. I ran a machine with Arthur and eventually I married his son, Ron. Once I started going out with him everything changed. I called my future father-in-law by his name at work but I couldn't when I started going up to his house. It was really difficult.

We lived with them for about five years after we were married and I still couldn't call him 'Dad'. I looked after both his parents until they died but never called them Mum and Dad. My parents were the only ones I'd call that.

DAILY EXPRESS

No. 14,012 · Coast dim-out 9.55 pm to 6 am · WEDNESDAY MAY 2 1945 · Moon rises 2.36 am (Thurs) sets 10.30 am · One Penny

GERMANS PUT OUT THE NEWS EVERY ONE HOPES IS TRUE

Drum-roll heroics—then the build-up of hero-leader fighting to his last breath

'HITLER IS DEAD'

Doenitz goes on radio: I am your new Fuhrer

'GERMANY WILL FIGHT ON'

Express Radio Station

HITLER was killed at his command post in Berlin yesterday afternoon, according to a Hamburg radio announcement at 10.30 last night. Grand Admiral Karl Doenitz, not Himmler, is his successor, and Doenitz announces: "The military struggle will continue."

The radio gave no details of Hitler's reported death, and the authority for the statement rests entirely on Doenitz. This may be the beginning of the great Hitler Legend to build up the Fuehrer as a mystical German hero and martyr.

The last German reference to Hitler was in yesterday's German Command communiqué, which said: "In the heart of Berlin the gallant garrison gathered round the Fuehrer and herded together in a very narrow space is defending itself heroically against overwhelming assaults."

For an hour and a half Hamburg radio built up to the announcement, telling listeners to stand by for grave news. An orchestra played Wagner's "Twilight of the Gods."

'GERMAN PEOPLE BOW'

At last, after four rolls of drums, the announcer said: "It is reported from the Fuehrer's H.Q. that our Fuehrer, Adolf Hitler, has fallen this afternoon in his command post

NOW WHAT HAPPENS TO BERNADOTTE?

COUNT TO MAKE NEW JOURNEY

From E. D. MASTERMAN

STOCKHOLM, Tuesday.—Count Bernadotte, the Swedish peace emissary, arrived back in Stockholm early today after his contacts with the Germans in Denmark, and said he could not make a statement about his negotiations "until certain things happen."

The situation was "too delicate and critical."

He also said he expected to make another journey soon. He would not say where.

The count deepened the cloud of mystery which covers his mission

OBITUARY

THE Daily Express rejoices to announce the reports of Adolf Hitler's death. It prints today every line of information about the manner of his death.

It wastes no inch of space upon his career. The evil of his deeds is all too well known.

It gives no picture of the world's most hated face.

It records that Hitler was born Schickelgruber at Braunau, Austria, on April 20, 1889, and that his days upon the earth he sought to conquer were too long.

HITLER II.

Himmler split from the navy?

By GUY EDEN

TWO questions to which British leaders were seeking answers after Hitler's death was announced were: (1) Does Doenitz, who has a reputation of being a tough warrior, intend to carry on a naval war from Norway? (2) How does the change from Hitler to Doenitz affect the peace effort being made by Himmler?

Conferences of Ministers, including Mr. Churchill, went on far into the early hours this morning. The Service chiefs were also in consultation.

Even close students of German affairs seem to have been

DEMOB. PLANS SPEEDED

First out six weeks after VE Day

By TREVOR EVANS

THE Government has decided to speed-up the first release of Forces men after Germany has surrendered.

When plans for release and resettlement were made last winter it was intended that a stop of three months would be placed on all in the Forces.

Two months ago the machine was geared up to enable a start to be made on releases within nine weeks of the end of the European war.

Now it has been decided to let the first men out within six weeks of VE Day.

Instructions for this have been sent to all headquarters overseas, so that the men affected can be assembled for transport home to enable simultaneous release of all men in the same groups.

The volume of releases will depend largely on how German garrisons in Norway, Holland and Western France respond to

Victory night— bonfire night

Express Staff Reporter

NEWS of the end of the war in Europe will be announced on the radio by Mr. Churchill, says a Home Office statement.

At nine o'clock the same night the King will broadcast to his peoples.

The statement warns that "the arrangements might be subject to revision if the end of hostilities took the form of a declaration by the Allied Powers that organised resistance had ceased."

Here are some of the things that the Home Office suggest should happen on VE Day:—

CHURCHES: Bells to be rung throughout the country. Churches of all denominations to hold special services and remain open for private prayer.

HOLIDAY: VE Day and the following day to be public holidays.

THANKSGIVING: The Sunday following to be observed as a day of national thanksgiving and prayer. Special services to be held in London, Edinburgh, Cardiff and Belfast. The King will attend the London service probably at St. Paul's.

LIGHTS: Because of the shortage of fuel and labour full

Edna and Bill Tomlinson.

'Can you fetch a cup of tea for this man? He's come for his job.'

I was the tea-girl and I used to take a cup to each man in the factory. They all had their own cups. I went off to get another cup and brought it back for him. There he was, still in his uniform even though he'd been de-mobbed. Once he was working with us he started pestering me to go out with him. On and on — and that was it. I've been fetching his tea ever since.

" We don't want another war but if ever there was one I'd put my name down to go back to Collaro's and work there again. "

The Collaro workers settled back to their lives. Some became parents, grandparents, even great-grandparents. Many of them still live in the area where all those years ago they worked twelve hour shifts, dressed in their boiler suits and turbans, churning out the bullets. The Ritz where they cried their way through films and the Palais where they danced in their high heels no longer exist but friendships and memories are alive from one of the most important times of their lives; their Collaro Days.

" I had some very happy times at Collaro's with some lovely people. "

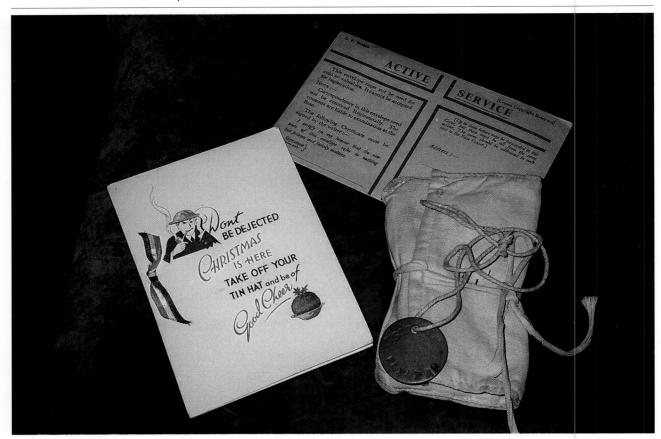